The CEO's Playbook

Play·book (pla'book') n. A book containing a set of tactics from which a winning strategy can be fashioned. A compilation of descriptions and diagrams of the plays of a team, especially a football team. A book containing scripts of dramatic plays.

The CEO's PLAYBOOK

Managing the Outside Forces that Shape Success

by

Ron Rhody

The CEO's Playbook
Copyright © 1999 by Ronald E. Rhody.
All rights reserved

Published by Academy Publishing, 3053 Freeport Blvd. #222, Sacramento, CA 95818

Printed and bound in the United States of America.

First edition

Academy Publishing books are available for educational, business, or marketing promotion use at special rates.

For more information, please contact:
Special Uses Department, Academy Publishing,
3053 Freeport Blvd. #222, Sacramento, CA 95818.
Phone (916)-736-2546

ISBN 0-9670679-0-1

Library of Congress Catalog Card Number 99-90193

THE CEO's PLAYBOOK

Contents

"IT'S A ROUGH GAME, SON. YOU GOTTA SUCK IT UP AND GO."

Explanation offered over the supine form of a freshman quarter-back bleeding lightly from the nose and mouth and dazed beyond comprehension after being blind-sided by a 260-lb. senior tackle in the first scrimmage of the year. Leo Yarutis, head coach, Georgetown College.

PREFACE

This book began as a series of memos to an exceptional young executive moving into the chief executive officer's chair at a Fortune 500 company.

I thought he wasn't prepared to handle a dimension of his job that could prove all important in a relatively short time. I wanted to help him get up to speed as rapidly as possible. So the memos began. They were followed by in-depth discussions that allowed him to test and argue and understand what he needed to know and how to use the tools at his disposal. I didn't expect him to become an expert, just as he was not an expert in finance or the law, but I knew he needed to be informed and educated on these matters so that he could manage wisely and not stumble unnecessarily.

From that experience, came this book. It is intended for those whose ambition and skills have them on their way to their own CEO's chair and those recently arrived who are beginning to realize the complexity of this other dimension they have to deal with.

The book is also for the owners and managers of the newer, smaller companies that expect to make their way in the market and who almost always find themselves facing these kinds of challenges with no experience in how to handle them and no staff to help with the solutions.

Middle managers who feel that knowing some of the things the boss has to know gives them an edge will find useful information here, as will those with growing responsibilities in the public and not-for-profit sectors who face many of the same pressures and for whom the same principles apply.

Over a long career I've worked for and with a lot of CEOs. Some were taller than others, some smarter. Some were spellbinders and a few so boring it was hard to keep a meeting awake. But they all came to a point in their careers where they realized that just knowing how to manage the business wasn't enough. They needed to know, as well, how to handle the outside forces that could constrain or advance their initiatives. None of them were trained for that. They were spending on average almost fifty percent of their time on these matters—about as much time as in actually running the business in the traditional sense. Some were very good. "Gifted amateurs" is the phrase used in sports. They had the feel and the touch for it, the presence and the intuition and the confidence.

Through them, and later as a private consultant, I came in contact with an even larger number of CEOs and senior executives. The situation was no different. Most were spending more and more of their time on matters not traditionally associated with "running the business." In fact, managing these non-traditional components had become a crucial part of the job. Many had talented Chief Public Relations Officers who were enormously helpful in handling these matters. Most, however, did not. Hopefully, this small book will help those without talented CPROs understand the game better and play it more effectively. Perhaps those with talented CPROs will realize what an advantage they have.

A note about gender references. Where the words he, him, or his are used in this text please take them to be my generic for all of us—for she, her, and hers. Writing he or she when referring to a single individual, or alternately using he and she, slows down the writing so much and seems so contrived, I opted to throw myself on the readers' good nature and hope for the best. I really do mean all of us by the term.

There is nothing magical in the chapter sequence. I have a certain flow in mind, of course, with one thing leading to another, but pick and choose as your fancy strikes you. The various points are self contained. The important thing is to read them all. You need to know this stuff.

When you've finished, I doubt I'd want to hire you as my Chief Public Relations Officer, but I'm certain I'll have much more confidence in your ability to prevail over the challenges of the new millennium. You'll know the game and have a better idea of how to play the hands that are dealt you.

I once asked a poker-playing buddy of mine, who seemed to win all the time, the secret of his success. He hemmed and hawed for a bit, then said with a smile I'll never forget, "All you need is a slight advantage."

May this book be a slight advantage for you.

Chapter One

TO BEGIN...

These forces make your world and you have to be able to handle them.

I have a steely-eyed chief executive officer friend who once thought that anything which didn't directly contribute to the making or selling of the product superfluous and was not to be tolerated. He didn't have time for all the foolishness associated with hand-holding, and cajoling, and otherwise inter-acting with the civilian world. He had a business to run. He ran it well until, alas, the environmentalists came knocking. And then the discriminatory hiring issue floated in. There was a problem about a chemical spill. A few big stockholders began to gripe about earnings not growing rapidly enough. He needed Congressional support for an expansion he wanted to make. *The Wall Street Journal* was nosing around about pricing. And so on and so forth did the outside world increasingly intrude until one morning my friend, the CEO, awoke to the notion that if he didn't start paying very serious attention to a host of forces he had felt the luxury to ignore or leave to others in the past, he might well wind up with no business to manage at all. His view of management priorities expanded dramatically.

The forces that brought him to this conclusion come in varying disguises:

- The news media, bless its heart.
- And the consumer and environmental and minority activists, who, if they think they can use you, will make your life a circus.
- And shareholders big and small, but mostly the big ones, whose bite can be much worse than their bark.

- And the people in the State Houses and on Capitol Hill and lurking on the staffs of the regulatory agencies watching and waiting.
- And the special interest groups that spring up around this issue or that, impassioned and determined.
- And your own employees whom you think you know, but don't.

These and all the other unruly, unawed, and unappreciative forces that derive from people—just people, singly and in concert, trying to get along as best they can in a world they never made– these forces make your world and circumscribe the environment you work in.

Very few managers ascending to their majority have been trained to handle any of them.

For the most part business schools ignore these forces. That so little is being done to prepare leaders for these challenges is almost criminal. Providing a CEO-to-be with the management skills and theory needed to run a successful business and yet not providing him or her with at least the most rudimentary skills and understanding of how to create buy-in from the stakeholders who will fund his vision, the employees who will make it happen, the governments who can stop him dead in his tracks, or the media who can sanctify or crucify his efforts seems to somehow be missing a very vital point.

Absent what the business schools do not provide, the little training most managers receive in these matters is done on the fly—some media exposure as you worked your way up the ladder, maybe a protest picket or two at a plant site, some conversations with security analysists, the obligatory visits to the state capitol or Washington to lobby your representatives and senators. And, of course, there is the acquired wisdom of your mentor group of older managers, the ones who've been helping you grow and shepherding your career—most of it more appropriate to the thinking of the 19th century than the 21[st,] and almost none of it responsive to the issues you have to deal with. I don't say this unkindly. They passed on what they'd learned from their mentors who had, of course, learned it from theirs in times when attitudes like "it's none of their business" and "my responsibility is to my shareholders" had more currency. That old mentality is bankrupt now. You're in a different game from the one they played. How to play it successfully is what this book is all about.

Aware of the time pressures you face, this will be as short as I can make it. You should be able to read it in the time it takes for the flight from New York to Los Angeles.

There is as little jargon as possible. The concepts are straight-forward. At the end there will be a suggestion for some additional reading if you are so inclined. When you've finished, you should have the basics of the information you need to manage the tools at your disposal.

So, to begin…

Chapter Two

CONCERNING THE PLAY OF THE GAME

The five givens.

This you can count on: things ain't ever gonna be the way they were, ever again.

No surprise there, of course. You've always known you have to be able to handle change. Change is the force that keeps things moving. When you don't get change you get stagnation.

What's different now, though, is the speed with which that change occurs. We've hardly time to grasp the one before the next is on us. And none of the changes seem inconsequential. One thing changes, a host of other things change. Pow! The dominos start falling. A new force rises where no one expects it!

Nothing very recognizable as evolutionary or orderly seems to be going on, or if there is, so much is going on so rapidly in so many different arenas we have difficulty seeing through the chaos. Wham! Bam! A new day dawning every second.

Or so it seems. Yet even in the midst of all this confusion and contention, there are certain truths that remain constant. Because they remain constant, they become givens. These are the givens:

- Perceptions are more important than facts.
- Performance almost never speaks for itself.
- If you want your story told right you have to tell it yourself.
- Timidity never won any ballgames and silence never swayed any masses.
- Without buy-in you can't succeed.

The five are inter-related. They are at work all the time in every situation. The ramifications of each are significant. If they are ignored, the price is considerable.

Chapter Three

THE FACT ABOUT FACTS

What you do may not be as important as what people think about what you do.

Facts are fickle. They stand ready to serve any master who can give them persuasive voice. They often serve several masters at once, sometimes several competing masters at once.

People don't pay much attention to facts. What they pay attention to is their understanding of the facts – their perceptions.

Politicians know this. Preachers and advertising people do, too, and demagogues, and activists and poets.

But very few executives do.

It's almost as if there is a flaw somewhere in the genetic code that makes it impossible to accept that people act on their perceptions, not on facts. It's not managers' fault, of course. All their training and education reinforces the idea that reason wins out. What really wins out is self. Each of us acts on the values we've fashioned for ourselves out of what pleases or frightens us, what rewards us or hurts us, what reassures or distresses us, what promises what we want or puts up barriers against our getting it.

What happens is that we run "facts" through our filters of self-interest and end up with a product different from the raw material we began with. We manufacture subjective facts, the facts the way we see them, i.e., perceptions.

The power in facts comes from the meanings that are given to them by this or that interest for this or that purpose. These meanings form perceptions and it is the perceptions that have consequence. What is important, then, is not so much the actions you take as the perceptions people form about those actions.

Perceptions are more important than facts

Chapter Four

A FEW RULES FOR DEALING WITH "FACTS"

Grist for the Mill of Perception.

- Don't assume that "facts" will carry the day. The only place unclothed facts have power is in the hard sciences and in the physical world. Everywhere else a "fact" is the tool of anybody who can give it meaning. That plant you're so proud of, that has state-of-the art environmental controls, the one that's providing substantial employment and paying substantial taxes—that plant can just as easily be seen as an insult to the environment and an impending threat to public health and safety. It depends on whose facts are being used—and how.

- Don't assume that logic will sway your publics. Jonathan Phillips had the right idea in his *Philosophy of Rhetoric* (1796). "To say that it is possible to persuade without speaking to the passions is specious nonsense." Persuasion has always been dependent on emotion, on the ability to appeal to the notions of right or wrong, fair or unfair, love or fear, helpful or hurtful, that we all hold. When organizations expect that the logic of their position will enlist the uncommitted and convert the heathen, they are usually disappointed.

- Perceptions can't be created out of smoke. Oh, they can for a while, but not for long and always with dire results. Remember Lincoln's line about being able to fool some of the people some of the time, but not all the people all the time? Eventually, the truth will out. You want to be right with it from Day One. When the smoke clears and people get a straight look at who you are and what you're doing, you want that image to be a mirror of the values you hold and the benefits your organization brings to its publics. Dissembling doesn't permit that.

▪ Remember that perceptions drive decisions and actions. Concentrate on managing perceptions. Don't let others (like the media, or government, or competitors, or critics) give *their* meaning to *your* "facts." If you do, you're dead.

A couple of examples where the facts didn't make much difference, but perceptions did.

Intel's introduction of its new super fast Pentium chip, the best and fastest at the time, seemed a world beating event. You'll remember that Intel had spent heavily in an attempt to connect with consumers with its "Intel Inside" campaign and had the public fairly well convinced that if Intel was inside, it had the best. The company was lauded and the new chip highly praised – until an obscure user uncovered a relatively esoteric flaw and turned the launch into a disaster.

When the flaw was revealed, Intel took the position that the problem was unimportant—that it would surface only in a sophisticated mathematical calculation that less than one percent of users could possibly encounter. Intel declined to recall the chip or replace it. Media and public reaction was immediate. Outrage at what was perceived as a cavalier attempt to foist a flawed product on an unsuspecting public grew so extreme in such a short period of time that Intel had no alternative but to bow. At first the company offered to replace the chip—but only for users who could prove they actually had reason to use the arcane mathematical tool. This seemed a reasonable and fair solution to Intel. Fix the flaw for the people who might really be affected by it, but for all those others who were unlikely to ever encounter a problem, it wasn't broken, so why fix it? Never mind that people felt Intel had no right to shove a flawed product off on them merely because they weren't the mathematical elite. The public hue and cry at this piece of arrogance grew so loud that Intel finally decided to replace the chip for all comers – no questions asked. This was the correct decision, the one that should have been made in the first place, and as they implemented it, the furor died down.

The fact is that Intel's "facts" were exactly right from the beginning. The flaw was, as the attorneys say, deminimous. Only a few users would have occasion to do a computation that would bring the flaw into play, and Intel was taking care of those people.

But the perception was that Intel knowingly put a flawed product on the market, wasn't doing anything satisfactory about it, and if consumers didn't like it they could go whistle in the wind.

Intel still has bruises from that encounter.

Or consider the Bank of America tellers case. Riding high with record earnings and rapid growth after a dismal period of losses, Bank of America was in the process of completing what was at the time the largest bank merger in history with its acquisition of California rival Security Pacific. To reap the substantial benefits of the merger, drastic cuts were to be made in the combined staffs of the two banks, and a number of branches were to be closed.

BofA stepped on the land mine when the media learned, from a disgruntled employee, that a large number of tellers were being arbitrarily moved from full-time to part-time status and that, as a result, they would lose not only income but their medical benefits as well. This was at a time when the health care issue was at the top of the Clinton political agenda and consequently very high on the national radar.

The story was a reporter's dream: here was a big corporation rolling to a year of record profits with executive compensation packages soaring through the roof and it's caught abusing its least powerful employees by cutting their medical benefits in an effort to boost profits even higher.

It was true that a large number of tellers were indeed being arbitrarily moved from full-time to part-time status, but this had nothing to do with an attempt to reduce health care costs. It had to do with the bank's desire for flexibility in scheduling. The bank wanted a maximum number of tellers on hand at peak demand periods but only an absolute minimum in off-peak hours.

But the perception, fed by the media, was otherwise. The bank began taking intense heat. Customers didn't like the idea of the big guy taking advantage of the little guy. Eventually, the bank got its story across, but only after a painful experience. The only beneficiary of the affair was the media.

The point here is not how the two organizations handled their crisis, but how easily facts become grist in the formation of perceptions.

Chapter Five

THE USES OF SPIN

Getting your story told your way.

In less contentious times, the act of helping people understand what facts mean was a legitimate, necessary, and responsible, part of the communications process.

It still is.

Unfortunately, this once proper and honorable act has become associated with the art of political propagandizing—otherwise known as "spin." The word spin is now used, of course, to give the impression that facts are being manipulated for devious purposes, or worse—that the facts in question may not be facts at all, but only the clever fiction of some well-paid liar out to confuse and seduce us all...an altogether unsavory act. The use of the word itself is a form of spin.

Pity.

The act of helping people understand ought not be saddled with the kind of slimy connotation the word spin now carries with it.

If you tell your story truthfully, that's not spinning in the politically repugnant sense, it's leveling. If you offer your honest interpretation of what it all means, that's not spinning, that's being responsible. If you think what I've just written could be called spin, you're right. But the fundamental difference is, I'm not trying to con you. Or mislead you. Or seduce you. My intent is to give you straightforward information and explain to you why and how it can be useful to you.

You owe your constituents as much.

If, as in the Bank of America case, people are left to believe that low level employees are being deprived of needed health benefits so that management can boost already remarkable profits to even higher levels, then shareholders, employees, and customers are all ill served.

You have the right to tell your story and the responsibility to tell it correctly. You have the right and the responsibility to provide the interpretation, explanation, and context that allow people to understand what you're up to and what, as you see it, that may mean to them. And you ought not be timid about so doing for fear someone may think it "spin."

What BofA was really doing in the teller case was trying to get flexibility into its working schedule so it could give customers better service (customers appreciate better service, right?), become more efficient and more competitive (making the shareholders' investment more attractive), and provide stronger benefits to its full time employees (which should make employees happy, it would seem). That's where the spin lay. But the bank got no chance to "spin" its story. The media pre-empted it. Though reducing health care costs wasn't really a consideration, the media made health care costs the crux of the story. All of which serves as a very instructive example of spin at work.

The keys to this kind of exercise are timing and credibility. Remember, now, I'm not endorsing spinning in its nefarious connotations. I'm urging you to get your story told your way by using the techniques of explanation and interpretation that are legitimately yours to use.

That said then, and to repeat, the keys to getting your story told your way are timing and credibility – timing in the sense that you want to offer your most compelling interpretation at the time the event is unfolding, and credibility in the sense that your interpretation is reasonable and believable.

If your company has been raping and pillaging across the countryside, it is unlikely people will believe, regardless of how brilliantly you make your case, that you have only their best interests at heart. If you let someone else be first to point to what you're doing and give their meaning to it, you've a very big hole to climb out of.

Every action has consequences, of course, but not the same consequences for everyone. Some people will like what you're doing. Some won't. Most could care less—unless, and here's the catch—unless what you're doing somehow affects them or they're told it does. Then they care quite intensely.

Absent information to the contrary, most people are generally willing to accept explanations that seem reasonable or likely. Your best chance to capitalize on this happy circumstance is to get your version told before someone pre-empts you (recall the BofA experience). In almost all circumstances, this means you have to tell it first. When you do, you gain tremendous advantages. You take control of the information flow and when you have control of the information flow you get to set the context and establish the fundamental facts. You also get the initiative.

With a credible story and holding the initiative, the next priority is to make sure your story gets told *the way you want it told to all the people whose opinions or actions might make a difference.* Not someone else's interpretation – your interpretation. Sometimes you may need to by-pass the media to make this happen, but doing this is not as difficult as might be thought.

Another major challenge is to fashion arguments which appeal to the interests and values of your constituents. Arguments which you and your staff find compelling often miss the mark because your frame of reference and that of most of your constituents are so vastly different. You won't solve this problem until and unless you find a way to see your world from your constituents perspective. This takes a certain amount of humility, and a larger amount of objectivity.

The most important aspect of the whole exercise, however, is tell the truth!

Sometimes you won't want to tell all the truth—not because you're devious or manipulative, but for competitive, or legal, or negotiating reasons, you'll want to tell only as much of the truth as you have to.

Sometimes you'll want to highlight an aspect or two of the truth to produce a result you want, but ignore the rest because it doesn't serve your purposes.

Telling only as much as you have to tell is frequently necessary for legal or competitive reasons. The attorneys will push you to say as little as possible all the time with the advice that what you don't say won't hurt you. That misses the point. In real life what you do say is often all that can save you. Silence doesn't win many arguments.

Trying to bend the truth is dumb. Enough people will know the truth of the situation to make attempts at fancy footwork highly dangerous.

Trying to hide the truth is, in the long run, a loser's game. Set aside plaintiffs' attorneys, regulatory agencies, congressional committees, activists' groups, and the occasional disgruntled employee, it is axiomatic among journalists that if as many as three people know a thing it can be found out. All the major news organizations today have both the resources and the ability to find out almost anything they want to know – if they want to know badly enough. (Which fact led Henry Kissinger to conclude that "truth is often the best alternative.")

So if you have a story to tell, tell it straight. Tell as much of it as you can. And don't miss any opportunity to tell it your way.

If that's "spinning," then do so in the knowledge that religions wouldn't survive, or politicians get elected, goods wouldn't be sold or markets made, the course of business proceed or governments stand, without it.

Chapter Six

"HANDLING" THE MEDIA

It can be trumped, ignored, even fooled, but...

There is a story, probably apocryphal, though I wouldn't swear to it. In the early 1940's, a B-25 slams into the top of the Empire State Building. Fire and debris rain down on the streets of mid-town Manhattan. Police and fire sirens fill the air. Traffic is stopped all over town. Crowds gather as the dead and injured are removed by ambulance. The military commander of the area, surveying the scene from his command car, calls his Public Information Officer over, fixes him with a furious stare, and says, "I don't want to see anything about this in the papers tomorrow!"

Whether the General actually said that, the point is that an awful lot of people in powerful positions think that news is controllable – or ought to be.

It is true that the media can be used. It is true that the media can be trumped. It is true that the media can be ignored, and bypassed, and even fooled for a while. But the media cannot be "handled." There are too many bright people, with too much ego, too strong a memory, and too many agendas, to make "handling" possible.

But it is possible to *work with* the media.

Very few CEOs do this very well. Some are frightened. Some assume they need not. Some think it beneath them. For which reasons most CEOs hand the responsibility off to a subordinate and wash their hands of the matter.

Don't be one of them.

No other single outside force has so much power to kill a career or block an initiative as the media. Nor can any be more helpful. Attention to a force that potent is too important to be delegated completely.

Of course the day to day interface with the media should be handled by a professional who understands the media, speaks their language and understands their needs as well as your— someone whose judgment and diplomacy you trust enough to let him or her speak for you and your company. This can be your Chief Public Relations Officer or the appointed spokesman on the CPRO's staff.

But you have to be a player – you have to be involved.

Just as you make time for key security analysts, you have to make time for key writers and editors. Just as you make the effort to know your key customers, you have to make the effort to know your key media. Not all of them – just the ones with the most clout. Who are they? This varies from company to company but generally they are the one or two writers or editors with the most influential by-lines in your headquarters city paper or papers; the reporters who cover you for the *Wall Street Journal* and the *New York Times* (if your company is large enough or interesting enough or there are bureaus close by); the key writer at the most important trade publication in the industry; and at least one solid relationship at one of the big business/financial periodicals like *Fortune, Forbes*, or *BusinessWeek* (again, if your company's size or potential merits their attention).

For smaller companies, don't give up on the *WSJ* or the *NYTimes* or the big business magazines. If you're doing interesting things and have potential you think they ought to know about, make the contact anyway. At the very least it'll give notice you're on the playing field.

Note that there isn't any mention of publishers here. Publishers are influential people. They don't, however, make news decisions. Editors make news decisions. When publishers try to make news decisions for editors, editors become very angry. The publisher's job is to run the business side of the paper. Editors run the news side. Though this distinction is beginning to blur as the business side gains more power from the pressures to rake in more profits, editors still take considerable umbrage when the business side tries to stick its nose into the news side. Publishers are likely to want to be your friend. They want your advertising dollar. Be their friend. They are usually urbane and interesting people with excellent contacts who entertain magnificently. Just don't assume they will be of much help when the chips are down.

They'll listen politely to your woes, but will maintain insistently that they never interfere with the editorial side of the house – bad policy, don't you know, a free and unfettered press sort of thing.

Notice also that there isn't a broadcast outlet like CNN or the Financial News Network in this list, or a wire service like Reuters or Bloomberg. All are important, but in a world of limited time, your personal focus ought to be on highly respected print outlets that help set both the tone and the agenda of subsequent coverage by other media.

If the *WSJ* thinks you're the hottest thing since sliced bread, odds are most of the other media will be inclined to look at you in a more favorable light, too. If your major trade paper thinks you've got the product or service that's going to stand the competition on its ears, the security analysts who regularly read the trades are going to be very interested. The beat reporters at the business and financial publications, who also mine the trades for story leads, will be, too. The Dow Jones news service (sister of the *WSJ*) and the *New York Times* wire service feed their copy to thousands of other media outlets around the world constantly and these outlets, in turn, influence other newspapers, magazines, and broadcast stations almost everywhere.

Concentrate on the key five. It will be the most time-effective initiative you take.

Chapter Seven

THE KEY MEDIA AND WHY THEY COUNT

An unconventional approach to the agenda setters.

In circumstances of material importance to the organization's success or survival – from take-overs to earnings shocks, from executive purges to major restructuring and all things of substance between and beyond – the *Wall Street Journal* and the *New York Times* are the most likely to do the in-depth reportage and critical analysis on breaking stories that carry the most authority with the most important constituents of American management.

Your board of directors will care about what the *Journal* and the *Times* say. So too will major lenders and the people who make a market in your stock. Shareholders and regulatory agencies and competitors will pay attention, as will your largest customers and your peer group of senior executives around the industry. Coverage in either or both of these dailies will stimulate coverage by other media and the slant they take will influence the slant others take – wire services, other dailies, the magazines, the broadcast outlets – and set the tone for the stories that ultimately the broader public sees and hears.

The headquarters media, the "home town" media, are important because these are the media with the most direct impact on the people you live and work with every day and whose approval underscores the firm's reputation and importance in the community. Some of your best customers, your largest stockholders, and your key employees will be regular readers, not to mention your wife and family (and their friends) and the guys you play golf with. What the local media have to say about you and your firm to these audiences has a consequence that far overshadows circulation figures or national stature.

The trade press is read mostly by your competitors and the people who want to do business with you—and, if you are a commodity type business, your customers. These are important constituencies, but the real importance the trade press holds is the role it plays as a source of knowledgeable information. The security analysts who follow your company read it. They get leads, assimilate arcane information, add bits of knowledge to the general store from which they draw their conclusions. The best reporters at the national dailies and magazines do likewise. As do investment bankers. And the staffs of regulatory agencies. And anyone researching your firm for this reason or that. Your own managers are also an important audience, and for the wrong reasons. Often, much of what middle managers know about what's going on in the company – the really important stuff that senior management doesn't feel middle managers need to know, or should know just yet – comes from the trade press. It's so much more effective to tell your managers yourself rather than letting the trade media spill it for you. But many companies still don't. Which is both sad – and dumb. But that's another story.

So trade press earns a spot on the list.

As for the big business and financial magazines, the *Fortunes*, *Forbes*, and *BusinessWeeks* of the world, they are tremendously influential. With more time to devote to developing articles and fewer inhibitions about objectivity (there are precious few anywhere, but the daily media at least makes a nod in that direction), the features and covers the big magazines turn out can have serious impact on a company, a product, and even on the tenure of senior executives. More than one CEO has been ushered out of the board room and out the door as a result of a criticism or revelation in a story in one of these magazines that stimulated a closer look by the board at the CEO's stewardship (or confirmed an impression the board already entertained). And more than one CEO owes at least part of his selection to a favorable story or stories that drew attention to his achievements and attributes in a way nothing else quite could and either prompted the promotion or brought head-hunters in with an offer from another company too good to refuse.

Yes, these are the traditional media, but I am suggesting you go about working with them in an unconventional way.

Let me be clear here that I'm talking about where your personal focus should be. Your media relations people may have a hundred or more key media they regularly deal with on a local, national, and international basis. From time to time they'll call on you to help out with one, or many, of these. Do it. You won't be asked unless it's important.

And yes, new media like the Internet are assuming an importance only dimly grasped at present. Already key media pick up leads and ideas, and angry employees and irate customers can trash you to all the world with ease and no expense. The Internet offers so much potential for mischief – and gain (the intelligence gathering aspects of the Net are staggering) that your PR people ought to be monitoring it (and the other developing media) constantly.

But as for you, keep your personal focus on your key five.

Chapter Eight

WORKING WITH THE MEDIA

If you don't play, you can't win.

The time and effort put into getting to know, and be known by, a core cadre of key media people can be one of the best investments you'll ever make.

This can't be a casual exercise. You need a carefully planned initiative. First, the really key media people must be identified and their backgrounds researched. You'll want to know where they come from, where they went to school, and what studies they pursued. You'll want to know something of their job history and of the stories they've written and of the style they employ (are they attackers, debunkers, tell-it-like-it-is types, or sensation seekers).

You'll want to examine, from past coverage, whether any biases are apparent.

You'll need to know where they are in the food chain of their publication and surmise to some extent their ambitions. And you'll want to know something of their personal situation (married, kids, etc.).

You're looking for common ground, for openings and land mines. Not that common ground will make much difference, but it can at least put initial contacts on a more comfortable plane.

You should make the contact with the reporter. Your CPRO could do it, but it will be far more effective if you do it yourself.

What I'm suggesting isn't the conventional wisdom. The conventional wisdom is that all contact with the substantive media come through your CPRO or his media relations staff. I was of a such a mind for years – made the introductions, sat in on the interviews, made sure all press queries were funneled through media relations. There is a decided advantage to this. If all media queries and contacts come through media relations, the boss doesn't get surprised by a reporter on the end of the line when he picks up the phone (secretaries are instructed to buck all media calls to the media relations people). So you don't run the risk of being put on the spot unprepared. In companies in the news a lot, the procedure also serves to regulate the amount of time the boss must spend with the media. Most importantly, though, it buys time to figure out what the reporter is up to, which in turn provides time for you to be briefed and prepared before making the return call or sitting down for the interview.

These are real pluses.

Even so, the advantages of solid working relationships between the CEO and selected key media people outweighs the risks. The major disadvantage of this approach is that you can't start ducking when things aren't going well. You have to stand in there in bad times as well as good.

If you follow this advice, it should go forward as a joint effort with your CPRO. Use his expertise to select the key five. Work with him on the best approach to be made. Keep him well informed and updated on what transpires. Strategize with him on the points to be made and how best to make them.

When you establish the contact directly, the reporter will be a little surprised (maybe flattered). That's fine. That's a plus. Nothing very complicated or involved is required. Simply tell the reporter what you have in mind and why—that his (or her) reportage is important to your company and to you and, consequently, you want to get to know him and give him the chance to get to know you. Be candid that you want to see if a relationship can be established that works for both of you—one in which the reporter knows he can come to you and get straight answers and one in which you know you can work with the reporter and get a fair hearing and more informed reportage.

Most reporters and editors will be happy with the prospect of having such an authoritative and influential source. Still, they're reporters, so they will be skeptical. Skepticism is part of the genetic make-up of reporters. This is neither good nor bad. It's the way they're trained (and in fairness, the result of experience). I grew up newspapering. My father was the first editor I worked for. This was on a daily in Kentucky's capitol city. He used to tell me, "Never believe what you hear and only half of what you see." He was talking mostly about political reportage, but it was great advice and is the sort of attitude most good reporters carry.

You'll have to go at this relationship much as you'd go at building a relationship with a key customer. Some things will be different. Whatever one may think about the standards and ethics of journalists (which on balance are usually as high as those of the people they cover) reporters are dead insistent to avoid anything which might give rise to the perception that their objectivity and independence are compromised. A number of major news organizations, the *Wall Street Journal* foremost among them, have policies forbidding their people from accepting perks like lavish dinners or theater tickets or golf outings or junkets to plant sites from news sources. The *Journal* either pays its own way or doesn't go. Consequently, and unlike the situation with security analysts and customers, entertainment isn't much of a contact building tool.

One of the strongest working relationships between a reporter and a CEO I've seen was established by nothing more than the simple courtesy of the CEO offering the reporter a ride home after a dinner meeting they'd both attended. It was a late night after a long day, the train schedule was spotty, and home was a little over an hour away for both of them. The reporter lived just a little further out than the CEO, but in the same direction. By the time the town car pulled up in front of the reporter's house, the two had a chance to talk quietly, get to know each other, and build a little trust. That trust got the reporter an authoritative source he would never have established otherwise, and while it bought no special treatment for the CEO, it always got him a fair hearing. In the best of all possible worlds, that's about the most you can ask.

No reporter or editor is likely to take you as advertised. You have to prove yourself.

You have to take and return phone calls, whether convenient or not. Reporters work in a world of real time. Deadlines aren't fungible. If one of your key contacts is on deadline on an important story and needs to talk with you within the next fifteen minutes, that means within the next fifteen minutes. Later won't do him any good. If the reporter is working a story and calls needing your input but you're out of town, you need to return the call anyway, regardless of the time where you are, or make sure someone does and lets the reporter know you'll get to him as soon as you can.

You'll not only have to be accessible and responsive, you'll have to make the effort to know the reporter personally. Working breakfasts or lunches are good for this. They are arranged as background sessions. Their purpose is to build relationships and provide information and perspective that can help the reporter do a better and more informed job of analysis and reportage, on both your institution and the industry overall. You update the reporter on what you see as important developments in the company and the industry and are looking for any observations the reporter has on the same. These are understood to be non-news sessions. They are done "on background" (about which more later).

Most reporters (certainly all the good ones) really do want to be as informed as they possibly can. They want to write intelligently and with authority. Not one among them wants to make a dumb mistake, say a stupid thing, or reveal how little they truly know to people who are really knowledgeable. If the reporter isn't informed, that is as much your fault as his. If he makes mistakes because he's ignorant or says stupid things because he doesn't know any better, part of the responsibility is yours. It is up to you and your staff to educate him, to make sure he isn't ignorant about your business, doesn't draw stupid conclusions by default. You're not his whole universe. He's got only so much time (and in almost all circumstances it's too little) to invest in understanding you.

Help him. Help yourself.

If you don't play, you can't win.

Chapter Nine

WHAT THE MEDIA IS AND ISN'T

Out to get you?

Perceptions in the executive suite about the media very often border on paranoia.

- They're out to get us.
- They don't understand our business.
- They're all a bunch of liberal, anti-establishment, sensation seeking wackos who'll twist our words and print any rumor that any nut cares to offer.
- They aren't smart enough to really understand what we're trying to tell them.
- They only print bad news – if it's something positive, they're not interested.
- You can't trust them.
- You wouldn't want your daughter to marry one.

Actually the media is not out to get you. Quite the contrary. The men and women who gather and write the news are out for fame and fortune—just like you. You do it by delivering constant increases in earnings for your shareholders and keeping the stock price high. They do it by ferreting out stories strong enough to get them by-lines and by being first with the news, or the revelations, or the judgment.

Being a really good reporter or editor takes a certain kind of mind and a special kind of drive—an insatiable curiosity about things; an irreverence for authority and power; a skepticism, not always pugnacious, but always penetrating; a strong IQ; a knack for getting people to open up, either through guile or intimidation; a sense that the big guys will always take advantage of the little guys if they can, which is to say a considerable distrust of bigness; an ability to explain things in ways that people can understand and react to, and in almost all cases, a very strong ego.

They like to think they are they public's surrogate and protector. In many cases they are.

They feel theirs is a noble calling (which it sometimes can be) and that, in the public interest, they have a right to whatever information they want.

Their talent for taking what to you may seem the most ordinary action or inconsequential piece of information and blowing it into something that gets people excited or upset is a defining characteristic.

They have imagination.

They are analytical and they draw conclusions.

They march to their own drummer.

But they are not out to get you…necessarily.

Quite simply, the media is a business. Its product is information and entertainment. As with any product, a raw material is needed. You and your company are raw material. The extent to which media can take the raw material your actions furnish and shape them into something people find interesting or useful, or something people ought to be concerned about, to that extent you're worth mining.

A good rule is if you don't want media nosing around, don't let dumb things happen that are likely to draw attention—things like letting the board give you a big raise just as a massive lay-off is being announced, as happened with the CEOs of AT&T and General Motors to great criticism and outrage.

An even better rule is try not to do things you'd be unhappy to see reported in a Page One story in the *Wall Street Journal*. If an action is being considered that can't stand public scrutiny, it ought not be taken. If it is taken, then bet on it that the media will be out to get you just as soon as they find out.

The news media is a business composed of relatively normal people trying to get along and get ahead like everyone else. They are neither the avenging sword of God nor the fount of received wisdom. Most are reasonable, responsible, and, to their minds, fair. The field certainly has its share of the arrogant, the egotistical, and the insufferable, and it definitely puts a fearsome power in the hands of sometimes inexperienced and irresponsible people, but as a whole, the news media is indifferent to whether you, or your institution, succeeds or fails.

The good ones in the media understand your business and are plenty smart enough to understand what you're talking about. Their educational background is generally as good as most of the people you have on staff and their IQs no worse.

Though they often print assertion and rumor, they do try to verify the credentials of those feeding them the information to determine if what is being rumored seems half way plausible.

Sadly, bad news makes more compelling reading than good news so that's what gets the most play. Bad news is also easier to write than good news. Still, if there is a positive story to be told, and a good enough case can be made for it, it will at least get a hearing and perhaps even decent play.

As for your daughter, let her make up her own mind.

Chapter Ten

GETTING TO MARKET WITH THE MOST ATTRACTIVE PRODUCT AT THE LOWEST POSSIBLE COST

Or how you and the media paddle similar canoes.

In late 1980s and through the '90s, media organizations everywhere went through the same sort of trauma corporate America experienced. There were mergers, acquisitions, drastic lay-offs. Many fine old names in American newspapering couldn't make it any more and closed their doors. Many two-newspaper cities became one newspaper cities. Big main line corporations began buying up television outlets and publishing enterprises, melding them into media conglomerates with enormous competitive potential. And a real premium was put on the bottom-line. Reporters and editors usually didn't pay much attention to the bottom-line and if they did at all, thought it didn't have much to do with them. Profits were something the guys on the business side dealt with.

No more.

After the lay-offs and the closures, reporters became aware that profitability equates to jobs and pay raises, and that profits come from the ability to deliver the kind and numbers of readers and viewers advertisers will pay to reach. Therefore, do what's necessary to get readers and viewers.

The business has always been brutally competitive, but the pace of change and the intensity of the battle for readers and viewers in the early years of the new century will make the last twenty years seem like a holiday.

Consider the competition.

There was a time when newspapers felt they were competing with other newspapers and magazines with other magazines. They all had a niche. They knew who they were and they had loyal followings. Then radio began to intrude a bit, and then television, and then came the explosion of television networks and channels pushing out so much stuff about so many things from so many places that nobody quite knew how to react and everyone started scrambling to carve out a special identity to distinguish themselves from the crowd and keep their circulation and ratings up.

To deliver the audience advertisers want, a newspaper or magazine or TV network has to have stuff that grabs people. They have to have it first—and if they're not first, then they have to make what they have more authoritative, more confrontational, more entertaining, or more sensational than the other guy's. Fail to do this and they begin to lose readers and viewers—which is all they have to sell.

Media runs essentially on advertising revenue. Advertisers (that's you and your peers) pay media to provide a vehicle through which they can deliver sales messages to large numbers of potential buyers at the most efficient costs. The fewer potential buyers, the fewer advertising dollars. The fewer advertising dollars, the lower profits. The lower profits—well, we know what that portends.

Fueling this already fierce competition is the potential for instantaneous access to almost any information almost anywhere at almost any time. Technology makes this possible. Competition makes it mandatory.

Which, in turn, has changed and is continuing to change the way news is reported and distributed—changed even the meaning of "news." Already the line between the real and the imagined, the actual and the staged, has blurred. More and more, the substantive gives way to the sensational; the authoritative succumbs to the titillating. The net of this is skepticism and distrust. Who can be believed? What can be believed? Absent a certain trust on the part of the public in the credibility and honesty of their institutions, suspicion and uncertainty thrive. In such circumstances neither the public nor the corporate interest is served.

The willingness on the part of the media to compromise news standards in service to the bottom line, just as companies compromise certain values in the same service, is a sickness that won't be overcome until the pressures to drive every last dollar of profit down to the bottom line as rapidly as possible abate somewhat. Is this likely to happen in the new millennium? Think it's likely to happen in your business?

A *Wall Street Journal* bureau chief told me they don't feel their competition is the *New York Times* or the business publications like *Fortune* or *BusinessWeek*. They think their competition is television...that by the time they get in print tomorrow morning with a substantive story that breaks today, their readers will have already been exposed to it three or more times through television. For the *Journal* to make their story compelling they have to have something newer, more confrontational, more sensational. Which effort, of course, can escalate an ordinary story into a banner. Or worse, keep a story that should have died yesterday alive for a punishing time. These pressures are getting worse.

All of which is to say that the media is a brutally competitive industry in the throes of a technological and process upheaval unlike anything it has ever experienced. Its individual members, if they are to survive, must get to market with the most attractive product possible at the lowest possible cost—before the competition.

Not unlike your situation.

If the media is seen in this context—as a high pressure business manned by people who make their way on the basis of their ability to generate material that will hook and keep an audience—you can begin to understand why they do some of the things most executives find so unsettling. Understanding how they must go to market, you can understand what they want and need. Out of that understanding, you can build a relationship that works for you.

Chapter Eleven

THE RULES OF ENGAGEMENT

On-background, off-the-record, no-comment and other curious dodges.

Every game has its rules – even this one. You want to make sure you have the rules straight and that you and the reporter you're dealing with have the same understanding of what they mean.

For your purposes, the three most important rules are those involving *on the record, off the record,* and *on background.*

On the record means that any and everything you say may be used and may be attributed directly to you. 'We're going to make a ton of money this year,' John Smith, chief executive officer of This Corporation, said today," or "Smith said the SEC investigation is poppycock and those people ought to find something better to do with their time."

Off the record means that nothing you say may be used per se.

On background means that what you say may be used, but not attributed to either you or your company. This is the infamous "knowledgeable sources" finesse. "A source close to the negotiations said today that This Company is close to closing the deal with That Company," or "Knowledgeable sources report that This Company's venture into some new product line is causing horrendous management and manufacturing problems."

While these definitions are the generally accepted meanings with U.S. media, don't take a chance on any misunderstandings. Have your media relations people or CPRO hash all this out before a media encounter begins.

If every thing you say is *on the record*, there should be no problems. *On the record* is where you'll want to be most of the time. It's the cleanest and strongest position.

But there will be occasions when *off the record* and *on background* are both useful and necessary.

If you tell a reporter something *off the record*, you do so usually to give him an understanding or an insight that will help him shape subsequent coverage – information which helps him be more informed in the questions he asks others or more accurate in his own reportage. You should understand, however, that if, by using information you've given "off the record," the reporter can ferret out that information from another source, he's perfectly free to use it—so long as you're not identified in any way. So never say anything you'd be troubled to see in print – even if you're speaking *off the record*.

The *on background* approach is the most useful tool in both the executive's and the reporter's kit. Its use allows a source to talk candidly and provide a depth of information not possible, or at least not wise or safe, if the source is to be identified. It is the Pandora's box from which all those wonderful revelations and juicy pieces of information attributed to "experts close to the scene," and "industry observers," and "knowledgeable sources" spring. Without it, the news business would starve.

Generally, I don't like to see CEOs going *on background* (this is sometimes called *for non-attribution*). If the boss has something to say it ought to be said on the record. If it can't be said for the record, perhaps it shouldn't be said. Still, there will be occasions when in order to help the reporter understand the significance of a move or the nuances of an action – to help him get the story right – *on background* has to be used.

One of the problems with *on background* is that it is inherently manipulative and therefore, a bit suspect. Reporters prefer everything on the record. They tolerate *on background* because it often produces substantive information not available otherwise – but they know that people who provide information and don't want to be named as the source may have motives that are not always pure...a little bump in the stock price, a little knife in the back of a competitor...all easy to do. And of course, there are times when reporters actively encourage *on background* – when they're on the trail of a major story and the only way to get people to talk is to promise them anonymity.

The CEO should use *on background* sparingly – but use it. It is sometimes the only tool that can make, or save, a major story on a matter vital to the organization's interests.

There is one other "rule" – the *no comment* rule.

Lawyers love it. Most of the "it's-none-of-their-business" school of executives cherish it also. The media hate it and will draw conclusions each time you use it. *No comment* to the media usually means guilty, as in…

Question: "The word on the street has it that you're in negotiations with XYZ Company. Are you?"

Answer: "No comment."

Conclusion: "Damn right they're in negotiations with XYZ Company."

A sort of folk logic is at work here. If, goes the reasoning, you're not doing something, why not say so? What's being hidden? Ergo, *no comment* equates with guilty in almost all circumstances and at almost all times. *No comment* is seen as stonewalling, as being evasive. The *no comment* rule boils down to this: if you want to be sure that people believe you're up to something, just give the *no comment* response.

Rather than say *no comment*, even when that's what you mean, try "I'm not going to comment on that" and give a good reason why – like "We consider all sort of opportunities all the time, some of which pan out and some of which don't. So I've taken the position I'm neither going to confirm nor deny speculation about what we might or might not be considering until such time as we have something concrete to report. When, and if, we do have something to report, you'll be among the first to know."

Sure, that's a *no comment,* but it's a *no comment* with enough context to let the reporter know you're not stone-walling and reasonable enough to raise some doubt.

No comment is an arrogant, off-putting, defensive phrase. You'll get a lot more respect and a much better press if rather than telling the reporter to stuff it, which is essentially what *no comment* tells him to do, you tell him why you're not going to tell him. There may be legal reasons, competitive reasons, reasons of confidentiality, all sorts of reasons.

Reporters love reasons. Give them.

You should also insist that if the reporter is going to use your response to such a question he quote you exactly. Not "Smith wouldn't comment on...," but "Smith declined to comment consistent with his practice of not commenting on rumors," or whatever.

Yes, you can insist that a reporter quote you exactly! That's another one of the rules.

Okay. You're *on the record* most of the time. You go *off the record* rarely. You use *on background* surgically, at key times to make sure the reporter has the story right. And you never say "no comment." At the very least you say "I'm not going to discuss that, and here's the reason why."

One final thing in this regard. Never assume the reporter knows you're talking *on background* or *off the record*. Announce the fact each time you choose to do it and make sure the reporter understands. Having an *off the record* or *on background* comment attributed and printed is a situation you don't want.

There is one other rule of engagement you want to consider. This one's unspoken. It works only one way. This is the rule: take care of your key reporters.

Few things are more damaging to a reporter's career, or more bruising to his ego, than to get beat on a story he should have had, or to miss an important angle he should have known about. When this happens he gets chewed out by his boss and laughed at by his competitors. Reporters have remarkably fragile egos. They also hold grudges tenaciously if they think they've been mislead or misused.

But more than ego and pique are involved here. Reporters make their reputation (and consequently their careers) by being first and by being knowledgeable. Those that are not don't progress very far.

So take care of your key reporters. Don't let them get beat or walk around dumb if you can avoid it. What goes around, comes around.

Chapter Twelve

PRESS CONFERENCES

Show time at the circus.

Napoleon once observed that he would rather face an army in the field than a gang of reporters asking questions. A gang of reporters asking questions is a fairly good description of a press conference.

Tom Clausen, former president of the World Bank and the man who led Bank of America through what was called by some the greatest turn-around in the history of banking, didn't share Napoleon's view. Clausen by far preferred press conferences to interviews. His reasoning went like this: in an interview, there are only you and the reporter. He has you all to himself. Without a competing batch of other reporters also trying to ask questions, he can keep boring in on a single line of inquiry, which, if not a subject Clausen cared to get into too deeply, could lead to one or the other getting frustrated or worse. In a press conference, though, there is maneuvering room. If Clausen didn't like the question, he could, in that great imperial way he had, give it an ambiguous reply and move on to the next questioner—and hopefully more comfortable ground.

Press conferences have their uses, but for the most part they are overused and CEOs should be players in them only in the most carefully chosen situations.

Editors and reporters prefer to get their news exclusively—and first. Few find press conferences very satisfying in this regard. And press conferences generally are anticlimactic, that is, they are usually called to confirm something already known or widely suspected and to give the principals the opportunity to flesh out details a bit.

The tool is used most frequently, however, when there isn't much real news to impart and the organizers hope that a little glitz and glitter, a meal or a few drinks in a toney setting, will generate attention that otherwise wouldn't be had. If an editor invests limited resources in sending a reporter to a press conference and the reporter invests the time in attending, the odds are that the reporter will find a way to scare up a story and that the editor will find a place for it in print – a sort of faux news event with all the players cooperating in the illusion that something important happened.

That the tool is still used so frequently means it still works, but even so, a press conference involving the CEO should be staged only when there is really substantive news to be had—a situation in which there is breaking news of sufficient importance to call the key media together and give it to them at the same time and in the same way—from the top.

That's what press conferences should be for. They allow you to lay your message on all the important media at a single stroke, get your news out widely and uniformly, and get all the key questions handled for everyone at once. In hard news situations, there often is no better tool. There are dozens of instances in which there is an urgent need to get your case made to key media rapidly and collectively and the press conference is the tool to use—if you're setting the record straight, for instance, or in a crisis situation, or starting a product recall, or announcing a major acquisition, or explaining a major restructuring.

Depending on the subject matter or the volatility of the situation, press conferences can be high drama and downright abrading, or they can be high drama and great fun. A good bit of this depends on your attitude and manner. Under no circumstances can you loose your cool. There may be a horse's ass or two in the assemblage, but don't let it get under your skin. His peers will know him for what he is and discount his antics ... unless you bite, at which point you become vulnerable and who knows where the pack may roam if the smell of blood is in the air. Be calm and be polite. Don't get defensive. Give straight answers. Don't dance around or try fancy footwork. Be courteously assertive. Be in command.

Accept the fact that during press conferences, the substantive information sometimes gets lost in the maelstrom of questions that flow from both knowledgeable and uninformed reporters alike. Off the wall ideas get voiced. Misimpressions arise among those who don't hear an answer clearly, or who don't listen carefully, or don't understand. Sometimes the spokesman just gives a dumb answer.

Real skill and a modicum of luck are required to keep press conferences focused on the news you have in mind. You may think you're introducing a new product, but the reporter may see it as threat to the public well being. You may think you're introducing a new executive, but the reporter may see a palace coup.

An example of how press conferences can go awry:

Not long ago, a major US based multinational staged a press conference in London to announce a significant expansion in an economically depressed area of the UK. The expansion would create new jobs, pump money into the coffers of local businesses, bring in more tax income, and was solidly endorsed by both the national and local governments. It should have been a slam dunk solid plus story—a win-win for all concerned.

Enter the fickle gods of press conferences.

One reporter in a group that represented the cream of the UK business press expressed an interest in the price the expanded plant would pay for government supplied electricity (this happened to be a plant in which electricity was consumed in large quantities). The company had, naturally, secured concessionary power rates—the standard sorts of concessions granted to anyone willing to put capital into the depressed area and create new jobs—and said as much. "Ah," says the reporter, "what have we here? A cozy deal? Is the company paying a fair price? If not, why not?"

And that was the story – it spun out on the question of whether the company had been handed a juicy deal. Never mind the new jobs or the boost to the economy, the reporter saw the story as one of questionable concessions. That reporter's spin dominated the subsequent play of the rest of the media and all those nice pluses went out the window. Later, after the furor died down and it became clear the concessions were appropriate, everyone calmed down and the company went successfully ahead with its expansion. That the concessions were fair and proper didn't make much news, the net of which was that most of the reading public was left with the impression that something a little out of order was probably going on and rather than the solid plus the company thought it had in hand, it wound up with, at best, a minor minus.

The company was under no compulsion to stage a press conference. There were other, less risky ways of getting the pluses out. But it opted for the traditional. And maybe it was just unlucky. That the CEO wasn't part of this exercise was about the only fortunate break the company got.

Still, the press conference is the tool to use when it is the tool to use. If the decision is to stage one and to involve the CEO, this is the check list you should use:

- Know the objective. No press conference should be staged without a clear fix on what message or messages you want to drive across. The press conference isn't being staged to give reporters a chance to ask questions. It's being staged to give you an opportunity to make your points.

- Know the players. You should have a good understanding of who from the media will be there, which ones are likely to be the most knowledgeable, and which are likely to be the most critical. Your CPRO can provide all this.

- You should have at least a mental picture of the staging – of the look of the room, of where you'll be relative to the audience; if others are involved, how and where they'll be placed. When you enter the room you want to enter it as if you're know what you're doing and are in command.

- Make your remarks and take questions standing. Many like the informality of being seated, particularly if the group is small. I don't. The standing figure projects more authority, offers more presence. Take advantage of all the pluses available.
- Role play the Q&A with your CPRO. He'll be able to anticipate the essential questions the media are likely to ask. Have him phrase them to you. Respond. Frame the answer and speak it. Don't say, "OK, I've heard the question. I know how to answer it. What's next?" Take the time to try out your answer. It'll probably be great. But it might be awful. A good CPRO will know what the press is likely to make out of what you say. He can help you make sure you're getting your point across and not shooting yourself in the foot. There will of course be off the wall questions that no one can anticipate. But be prepared for what you can prepare for, and make sure you get your messages across regardless of the questions.
- Don't elaborate unnecessarily. Answer each question as candidly and concisely as you can and then move on. Gratuitous information often causes unexpected and unnecessary problems. In an interview with the *Wall Street Journal* for a story on a conflict between partners over compensation, the CEO of a major consulting firm offered a dollar figure on the amount in contention. The CEO was making the point that the amount was small in context of the firm's overall income – "less than $100 million," he said. The reporter didn't ask for the dollar amount, was perfectly happy to accept that the amount was small in the scheme of things, but when the CEO volunteered the $100 million figure, bells went off. To most people, $100 million is a lot of money. At least the reporter thought so and played the story accordingly. What was being positioned as a minor conflict among colleagues became a $100 million fight over fairness. Rather than

making his case, the CEO unintentionally hurt it. Try not to answer questions that aren't asked.

- Have your own "reporter" in the room—someone from your media relations staff who takes down the questions as they're asked and writes down the answers, just as a regular reporter would. You'll want a record of the event—of who asked what and what your reply was. It is sometimes good to circulate this to key management and perhaps even members of the board so all have an understanding of what you said and the points you made. Not as a defensive measure, but so that all your colleagues have a clear fix on the position you've taken and can be consistent in their subsequent discussions with others – and most important, so they won't be surprised when they read it in the newspaper.

- Run it yourself. There are two basic ways to stage a press conference. In one, your CPRO, in effect, acts as the master of ceremonies. He enters the room first, introduces himself, tells the media briefly what to expect (i.e., who'll be speaking, that there will be a few minutes of opening remarks after which the floor will be opened to questions, and that everything is for the record). Then he introduces you (and your entourage, if any) all of whom enter, take their places, and you begin speaking. That's one way. The stronger way is to do it yourself. You enter the room, take the podium, introduce yourself and your colleagues. You thank the media for coming, tell them the subject of the session, that it's all on the record, that you have a few brief opening remarks, and that you'll then open the floor to questions. You control the meeting. You recognize the questioner, field the question or give it to one of your entourage, move on to the next questioner, etc. If it's a large media group with a number of unfamiliar faces, it's worthwhile to ask, as you start the session, that each questioner identify himself and his affiliation. They know who you are. You'd like a chance to know who they are and whom they represent (which lets you use the information from the earlier briefing on attendance). After you think the session has run long enough, or after it's obvious most of the questions have been asked, signal the end by saying something to the effect that, "We have time for one more question." Take it, give the answer, then wrap it up. Thank them again for their time and note that if they have subsequent questions they should get with your CPRO and he'll follow up with you. Smile and walk briskly out of the room.

Chapter Thirteen

ANOTHER WAY

When one on one is best.

If you have real news to make, and time to work it, the best tool isn't a press conference. The better tool is the rolling one-on-one.

This is the way it works:

A press release announcing whatever it is you have to announce is prepared and readied.

At a pre-set time, your media people call the key outlets (in this case your key five plus Reuters, Dow-Jones, Bloomberg, and AP) and tell them a major announcement will move within the next fifteen minutes (by whatever combination of wire, fax, and/or messenger your people use) and that the CEO will be available for the next few hours (say from 9:30 a.m. until noon) to take questions and elaborate on a one-on-one basis. If the reporter is interested (he will be), a time is set for the interview.

Let's say the release moves at 9:00 a.m. At 9:30 a.m. you begin a series of individual interviews with each reporter on the schedule. The interviews are done by phone (or face to face) at exact times set by your Chief Public Relations Officer with the reporter, i.e., the *WSJ* at 9:30 a.m.; Reuters at 10:00 a.m., etc. Your CPRO places the calls to the reporters and the interviews are done from your office. If you want colleagues involved—the Chief Financial Officer or the Chief Operating Officer, or a subject matter expert—they assemble in your office and the interview is done over speaker-phone.

Admittedly, a block of time has to be set aside for this, but not much more in aggregate then would be consumed in a press conference involving travel to and from an out-of-office site.

Everyone benefits. You get the chance to get your substantive information across in a non-circus atmosphere to knowledgeable reporters asking pertinent questions . The reporter gets exclusive time with you to pursue his questions uninterrupted by other reporters clamoring for attention. The result is almost always more responsible and better reportage

Part of the appeal of this approach is that, though the news may be substantive, the CEO doesn't always have to be involved. For example, when a *Fortune 100* company was ready to announce findings of an internal investigation into employee involvement in a scam that caused the company to take a multi-million dollar loss, the company didn't call a press conference, it used the rolling one-on-one technique. The senior investigator on the case and the company's senior attorney did one-on-one interviews with all the key national media—and got accurate, balanced, non-sensational coverage. Everyone was happy. The individual reporters got to put their questions to the executives with the most knowledge on the matter—and they got individual attention. The company officials got to make their case to responsible journalists in a low key atmosphere. The way the wire services and major dailies played the story set the tone for everyone else. When the company's yearly earnings were announced (the worst in years) along with a decision to cut the dividend, the same technique was used, but this time with the CEO and CFO – again with the result of balanced and responsible reportage.

In the real world, that's about the best you can ask.

Chapter Fourteen

INTERVIEWS

A game of wits you don't want to lose.

This is what you should remember about interviews.

Except in breaking news situations, and often even then, the reporter comes in with a definite story slant in mind. He's not there to gather general information from which a story will spring. Time is too precious a commodity and in too short supply. If an interview has been set, you can count on it that the reporter and editor have discussed what they think the story is and the reporter is there to get what he needs to support that premise.

Most of the time you won't know what that premise is. Sometimes you will and you won't like it very much, but if you are very, very good and the reporter's story premise is way off line, you might, with sufficient conviction, disabuse him of bad ideas. Getting someone to let go of an idea, particularly one he thinks is particularly revealing and one on which he and his boss (the editor) are of a like mind, is possible but chancy.

Forbes magazine thought it was on the trail of a hot story when it found, in routine SEC filings, that the CEO of a major multinational industrial firm had sold a large block of stock several weeks before a public announcement was made of a problem with one of its offshore projects which would cause a large hit to earnings. When, shortly into the interview, the reporter asked the CEO to explain why he sold the stock at such an opportune time, the CEO hesitated a moment then, smiling, said, "You may find this hard to believe, but like almost everyone else, I spend a little more than I make. I needed the money."

Nothing devious or underhanded, just a man getting money to pay his bills.

Luckily, the reporter heard the answer. Reporters on the trail of big stories sometimes don't hear very well. A filter kicks in. The points that support the reporter's premise come through clearly, but those that do not don't register quite as well. It's the nature of the contest.

And interviews are contests—games of wit and skill between interrogator and subject.

The reporter, if he's any good, will have done his homework. He will have read all the pertinent research, gone back over the key stories of the past months or year. He will have sought out employees, gruntled and otherwise; looked up cronies; and studied as much of your background as can be had from the public record. He'll have his questions well in mind and an idea of what he thinks the answers are – like a good trial attorney.

He'll also have an idea of how he intends to put them, and in what sequence, to get you to tell him what he wants to know, whether you intend to or not – like a good trial attorney.

He'll most likely come on friendly and reassuring, assuming that if you don't feel threatened he has a better chance of getting what he wants. A few reporters are abrasive. Some are confrontational – but that's mostly in situations in which the company is in trouble, or on the verge of it, and it's felt you're trying to hide something or stonewalling.

All good reporters have definite questioning patterns, just as good attorneys do – some weaving out a skein of apparently unrelated queries, jumping from this matter to that, alternating hard and soft questions, circling and collecting in no easily apparent order. Others come at it quite methodically, each question a building block in the case the reporter is trying to construct – no dodging and weaving, just the facts, ma'am. In the former you're never quite sure where the story is going (unless you ask). In the latter, it's fairly obvious.

Since interviews are one on one, the impression the reporter forms of you has a controlling influence on the tone of the subsequent story. Arrogance doesn't come across very well. Neither does impatience. Nor condescension. Inflated egos provoke an urge to puncture. Evasiveness suggests something is being hidden. Weakness invites attack.

Having said all this as cautionary, I don't want to leave the matter with the impression that interviews are necessarily uncomfortable, unsettling, or abrasive. Some can be, of course, but for the most part you're dealing with intelligent people who are interesting in their own right and from whom you can often learn as much as you reveal.

The contest can even be fun – if you believe in your story strongly enough. Look what the Apostles did with all those heathen.

Chapter Fifteen

MORE ON INTERVIEWS

Even in the most benign of cases there is a trial going on.

You should prepare for an interview as you would prepare for testimony at trial.

Most of the reporter's questions can be anticipated. Your CPRO or media relations people should be able to do this. They should know enough about the reporter, the publication, and the case the reporter is probably trying to make to be able to predict the questions that will be put to you. Often, finding out what those questions are is as simple as asking. Reporters are usually perfectly happy to let you know what areas they want to cover. They won't give the exact questions (or all of them, and there's the rub) but they will identify the areas that interest them most.

Just as in preparing for a press conference, you should role play the Q&A. Your media people should prepare a list of the probable questions. Those questions should be put to you orally and you should respond orally, hearing how the answers sound and working with it until you get it exactly right. Tuck the key phrasing of the "exactly right" answers away in your mind and bring them out when the questions come. It's unlikely the question will be phrased in exactly the language you've heard in rehearsal, but you'll recognize the thrust of it and you'll have the best answer ready.

Don't neglect to do this because even in the most benign of cases, there is a trial going on. The reporter, as the "people's surrogate," questions you on the public's behalf (shareholders, customers, etc.) about matters which presumably are of consequence to the publics you serve. It is incumbent on you, as the witness, to be at least as well prepared as the reporter, so that you can tell your story straightforwardly and convincingly. To do this, you have to be prepared. Which means you need to have a fairly good idea of the questions that are likely to be asked. You need to have firmly in mind your answers for those questions and how you plan to phrase them. If you think you're smart enough and knowledgeable enough to answer any question the reporter can put to you in the way that best makes your case and don't need to prepare – you're wrong. Taking such a stance is a matter of stupidity, ego, or a strongly ingrained death wish. People don't make it to the CEO's chair by being stupid. I never heard of one with a death wish of any type. But egos? Ah, egos. CEOs wouldn't be where they are without strong egos. That's good. That's given. But don't, please, let ego fool you into bad mistakes in matters of the media. What you say in an interview is on permanent file. It can be called up almost anytime and almost anywhere. Lexus, Nexus, any of the search machines on the Internet, or in the files of the various media – the most brilliant and the dumbest remarks are there to be found and referred to by any other reporter at any time present or future. What you say really can come back to haunt you.

To fail to adequately prepare for an interview should be as unthinkable as failing to prepare for testimony in a case of consequence. When you talk to a reporter from the *Wall Street Journal,* you're talking to almost two million people; to one from the *New York Times,* a little over a million; your headquarters city paper, tens of thousands at the very least. No one should approach those kinds of numbers, with the potential impact the opinions and actions this cohort of people can have, as if it is a casual exercise.

Not only should you have a good fix on the questions you're likely to get, you should also know enough about the reporter to understand what you're up against. The same rules that apply to press conferences apply here—in spades.

And don't forget the reason you're doing the interview. You're in it to get your story told. Anything else is a waste of time and a risk taken unnecessarily. Interviews shouldn't be passive situations in which you're there supplying answers on demand to inquisitive reporters. Interviews should be assertive situations in which you get your points across regardless of the questions asked. You should enter every interview session with a clear idea of what you expect to get out of it. You should know the points you want to make, how you want to make them, and then proceed to get them made. There are countless opportunities to do this in any interview. Sometimes the point you want to make can be segued to from an answer to another question. Sometimes you merely say something like, "That's an interesting question, but before I answer that one let me tell you..." Then go on and make your point.

I've likened interviews to games of wit or mini-trials. They are both. The thing to keep in mind is that, as in all games, skill, intelligence and confidence—with proper preparation—pay off. And as in trials, candor, credibility, and poise—with proper preparation—pay off. In both games and trials, there are winners and losers. There is no need to be the latter.

Chapter Sixteen

SILENCE, SUPPOSITION, AND OTHER GAMBITS

How to recognize the bait.

Not all reporters employ the same gambits in interviews, but there are a few techniques so standard that all use them from time to time.

One of the most effective is silence.

The reporter asks you a question. You respond.

Silence.

He just sits there looking at you – patiently waiting for more, as if your answer was incomplete, or unsatisfactory, or somehow lacking the candor and depth he has come to expect from you. You look back, waiting.

Silence.

You become uncomfortable. What's the matter? Didn't this joker understand what I said? How long can we keep staring at each other like this? Where's the next question?

Soon, to ease the strain, you start talking—maybe elaborating on the answer you've already given, maybe going off on a tangent suggested by something flitting through your mind. The reporter sits there sphinx-like still, and you ramble on even more expansively until you've said something you didn't mean to say, offered information you didn't intend to give.

Reporters count on that. They count on a subject's discomfort with a period of silence to work wonders in loosening the subject's tongue. Strong psychology is at work here. It relies on an implicit understanding that mannered people have an obligation to hold up their end of a conversation – to keep the dialogue going. If you don't (or can't), our social mores suggest, you're either rude or dull. By the time most of us reach adulthood the idea has been so firmly ingrained that it is almost second nature to abhor a gap of silence in an ongoing conversation. And so when you run into one in an interview, your social handler kicks in. "Fill the silence, you dolt. You want people to think you're dumb or something?"

Interviews aren't social encounters. If you've answered the question, don't keep elaborating just to avoid the sound of silence. Don't fall for the gambit.

Another approach sometimes used is to offer you the opportunity to comment on a generally outrageous or otherwise provocative remark supposedly made to the reporter by a competitor, an analyst, a customer, an employee.

Don't take the bait.

Any time you're offered the opportunity to explain your actions in response to a criticism (or a speculation) from an unidentified source, decline it. Don't react to nameless critics or respond to the conjecture of invisible parties – on the record. If you feel compelled to set the record straight or can't resist retorting to mindless speculation, use the off-the-record or on-background finesse. You can get your points made with minimum risk and reasonable effectiveness.

Often the statement the reporter wants you to respond to is offered merely as a tactic to see if there is any substance to the supposition. The reporter may give it very little credence at all, but tries it out to see how you respond and if you respond strongly enough, he's got a story.

Take the position in these instances that you're perfectly happy to respond to the valid criticism of any person or group responsible enough to be publicly identified, but that you're not going to play games with unnamed parties whose motives are probably suspect and whose access to substantive information may be limited to little more than conjecture and rumor.

Then go on to make your positive points about what's going on with the company and how all your constituents are benefiting from same.

Another gambit is the paraphrase. This is the one where you give an answer to a question and the reporter paraphrases the answer back to you, in his words, " So what you're saying is …" and then goes on to rephrase what might have been an extended answer into something shorter or more pithy. Most of the time the subject doesn't pay a lot of attention to the paraphrase and nods okay or says "yeah" and moves on to the next point.

Dangerous.

If you accede to the paraphrase, the reporter can use it as he's phrased it, not as you did. Don't let anyone put words in your mouth. If there is paraphrasing to be done, you do it.

And finally, there is the unchallenged statement gambit.

The reporter, in setting up a question, makes a statement or draws a conclusion about an action, or a result, or a person, with which you don't necessarily agree, but which you let pass in order to get to the question itself.

Never let these go by unchallenged.

The assumption the reporter draws in setting up a question becomes part of the premise. If you let it stand, he has no reason to assume the assumption isn't correct or that you disagree.

The net of all this is: be patient, be assertive, stay alert.

Chapter Seventeen

YOUR BEST INTERESTS AT HEART

Only your mother...

The best gambit of all, however, is the "it's in your best interests" dodge.

Usually it goes this way: a reporter is working a piece involving your organization, usually a critical piece, may have it almost finished, will have talked with your critics, has his story line well in hand and calls to say, "I'm doing a story on matter X for tomorrow's paper (or Sunday's, or whenever, but normally an issue date coming up soon) and wanted to give you a chance to comment on what I have. I think it's in your best interests to see me."

Count on it – the odds that what you have to say will substantially change the story are very low.

And count on it – no reporter or editor ever has your best interests at heart.

This ploy is almost always a not so subtle form of intimidation. "I've got the goods and you better talk with me or else." The reporter's mind is usually pretty well made up by this stage. Not much of what you have to say will make the story, and what little that does will only help validate the perception that the story is balanced and fair. After all, you've been given the chance to tell your side of it, haven't you? Of course you haven't. The only thing the reader will know of what you've said is those parts the reporter chooses to put in the story.

There may be many instances in your career when you find yourself in this situation – and many instances when, even though you know what the game is, you'll choose to play because being absent from the story may have greater consequences than being in it.

But not always.

Sometimes you will take actions you know to be in the long term best interests of your shareholders, your customers, or the organization's success, but which in the near term may draw fire from special interests, activists, even your customers. If that's the case, and you and your CPRO have concluded there's little chance of getting a balanced hearing in the story, there's no need to put yourself through the abrasion of a hostile interview with a prosecutorial reporter whose mind is made up.

Let him write what he plans to write and go on about your business. Odds are the story won't be an earth shaking event or be seen by the whole world.

If the story, though, is strong enough to get other media interested, make your points in the second day stories being done by follow-up reporters in other publications where you're more likely to get a fair and unbiased hearing. If no one's doing a second day story, and you think the issue substantive enough to justify a countering response, generate one. Have your CPRO get on to one of your prime contacts and get one going.

And – or – take your story directly to your key constituents in ways which we'll cover a little later.

The point is, no one has your best interests at heart but you (and maybe your mother).

Chapter Eighteen

BAD PRESS AND THE COMPANY'S BOTTOM LINE

Not nearly as bad as it seems.

Companies do dumb things from time to time – even bad things. It's the nature of the beast.

Quite frequently this leads to bad press.

But bad press isn't the end of the world.

Let's say, for instance, that the *Wall Street Journal* does a really bad page one piece on Company X and its antediluvian employment practices, or how it's losing its competitive edge, or whatever. The CEO reads the piece on his way in to work and has a minor stroke. He's embarrassed. He's mad. He wonders what his board will make of it. He knows his golfing buddies at the club will stick it to him. He's sure everyone in his wife's circle will have heard of it. He sees his sterling image as a leader of men and a master of commerce sullied. Customers, employees – what will they think of his leadership abilities and stewardship performance?

Bad stories are uncomfortable, but not the end of civilization as you know it.

The whole world will not have read the piece.

Many, if they read it at all, will recall it only vaguely.

And most won't care.

Instructive is a Bank of America incident. The bank knew a bad story was coming in the *San Francisco Chronicle* and, using political polling telephone techniques, was prepared to conduct an instant survey among readers to assess the damage. The story played as the major item on the business page that particular morning. Polling was done in mid-afternoon. The results? Of the readers of the *Chron* that day, less than fifty percent remembered seeing the story. Of those who remembered the story (this is the top story on the business page, remember) only about half could recall what it was about. Now clearly, the bank would have preferred that the story not have run. But having run, it was not nearly the event management thought it would be. Customers weren't canceling accounts. The public wasn't up in arms. Nobody was being burned in effigy.

What this suggests is that most readers of most newspapers don't read everything in them, maybe not even most of what is in them. And most readers of most newspapers don't really care very much—unless they are personally affected or involved. This goes in spades for radio and television. Most listeners don't listen very carefully. They're concentrating on the traffic, worrying about the upcoming meeting, involved in some other activity. They only half hear things (this is a real danger—a lot of mischief can be caused by what people think they heard, but didn't). And most of us don't give our full attention to television either, being otherwise engaged in flipping through a magazine, looking at reports, etc.

Not listening. Don't care very much. Not nearly as big a deal to them as to you. All the evidence leads to the conclusion that unless a story is about a material event that will hurt earnings or involves a threat to public health or safety, the near term effect on the bottom line will be nil.

I repeat, the near term effect of negative coverage on the bottom line is nil. Ditto the long term effect.

The story may be a little embarrassing and make you a little uncomfortable, but its impact on the thing most senior managers say is their principal concern—the bottom line—is unlikely to cause a minor blip.

This assumes, of course, that the story is a one-day story and is confined to a single publication. If the piece is picked up and replayed in a variety of media for an extended period of time, the impact on the bottom line may be considerable indeed. But even then not necessarily.

Consider the Exxon Valdez incident, Union Carbide and the Bophal disaster, the hits taken by General Motors on management compensation, Intel's chip fiasco, etc., etc., etc. These were all major negative stories that dominated media for extended periods and had serious consequences on the favorability ratings given these companies in public opinion polls.

Still, Exxon and DuPont and General Motors and Intel, and a host of other companies who've taken it on the nose for this failing or that, felt little impact to their earnings as a result of negative press play. And have apparently suffered no long term ill effects.

The moral of this story? A one or two day hit in a major media outlet isn't the end of the world. If you're big enough, and your products are in sufficient demand, even an extended run of negative media won't do much, if any damage, to the bottom line – unless of course, you are truly evil, in which case you should and will be found out and crucified. Absent that dimension, the thing to do is develop a little thicker skin and understand that media criticism comes with the territory.

Take note, though, that I'm talking about the *bottom line*, not the *stock price*. The near term impact of negative news about developments that directly impact earnings can be dramatic— knocking points off the stock price that can take months, in some cases years, to recover.

Chapter Nineteen

BAD PRESS AND YOUR BOTTOM LINE

The board may not be amused.

So you've bought everything I said in the previous chapter. You're developing a thicker skin. You understand that criticism comes with the territory. You're okay with the idea that a bad press day isn't the end of the world. That was the good news. Here's the bad.

▪ If spread broadly or repeated often enough, bad press can erode the organization's reputation. In the final analysis, all any organization has to sell is its reputation.

▪ The effect of negative stories on employees can be demoralizing, raising questions about management competence, about the direction the company's taking, even about the company's ethic and values.

▪ Even though there seems little correlation between negative press and the health of the bottom line, there is no way to calculate lost opportunity—the lost competitiveness from bright young talent who don't join the company because of negative press they've read; the lost revenue from new and potential customers who stay away because they're turned off by your alleged misdeeds; the lost potential from the deals that don't come to you because it's felt you can't be trusted. Or perhaps worse, the legislative or regulatory initiatives that are launched against you, stimulated by negative press.

What can't be measured is what might have been.

In a more precise sense, however, the biggest single impact of negative press for the CEO is with the board of directors. Boards don't like public criticism. They don't like it when their

CEO draws fire for poor management or questionable dealings or bad decisions. They don't like all that embarrassing attention. Even more, directors dislike the implication that their stewardship is faulty or their ability to see problems and fix them is weak.

The easy solution is to offer up a sacrifice. You.

This presents an interesting conundrum: bad press rarely has any significant impact on the bottom line, the vigor of which is the CEO's principal responsibility, yet bad press can have considerable impact on the CEO's tenure.

Here is what the wise CEO does to obviate this hazard:

▪ He educates his board members to the real impact of negative press on bottom-line results.

▪ He alerts at least a cadre of the most influential directors when he knows a negative story is coming and explains to them how he's handling it and why. This action takes away the suprise and buffers the shock of bad press and gives the directors something to use when asked by their colleagues or constituents about what's going on. They look informed, on top of the situation, in control. Very good stuff for directors.

▪ And the wise CEO takes his story directly to his key constituents (major shareholders and customers, his employees, legislative and regulatory contacts, community leaders, even his business peers when appropriate). He knows that if he wants his story told right, he has to tell it himself.

Chapter Twenty

GOING DIRECT

By-passing the media for fun and profit.

Since the beginning of mass media, it seems, business and industry have labored under the impression that they are at the mercy of the commercial media in getting their story told to the public. What else was there that could access mass audiences quickly and with credibility? If the media didn't carry your story, it didn't get told, unless of course you bought the story telling rights (called advertising) and had the media assemble the audience and deliver the message for you.

If the media did carry your story and it wasn't advertising but rather the sort of thing you'd just as soon never see in print, there was no way to get your side of it told unless you paid for the space – advertising again – which for purposes of setting the record straight, lacks both impact and credibility. So there you were, at the mercy of the commercial media.

No more.

The technology and the techniques now exist that enable you to take your story directly to those who matter. You can do this with credibility and impact and you can totally by-pass the media in the process.

All the tools the media uses are available to you now at affordable costs. Print, video, satellite broadcast, audio, the Internet and Intranets, and all the communications channels computers open up – with and through these you can reach your constituents directly with your full message...unedited and unfiltered by the commercial media. With the creative use of technology almost everyone whose opinions or actions can help you or hurt you can be reached directly. You don't have to depend on the media to carry your story for you anymore. In fact, you're behind the curve if you do.

Clearly these techniques won't deliver the mass audiences the commercial media can. But that's not necessary. What is necessary is to be able to reach the people whose opinions and actions can help you or hurt you. You want to be sure that, at the very least, they have responsible information on which to base their judgements, and at the very best, are persuaded to support your goals and actions.

To reach them, however, you must know who they are. This is becoming an increasingly easier task.

City by city, state by state, your people ought to be able to identify those whose opinions or actions make a difference—the people in the leadership circles in business and government, the civic and social leaders, the movers and shakers in the professional and service organizations and in cultural activities, the media elite. You already know the names of the key security analysts who follow you, and your key investors and shareholders. The leaders in the special interest and activists groups in your orbit should be easy to name—even the company's major critics. In all but the largest consumer products companies, big customers and clients will be on your marketing managers lists. And your employees—you're surely able to name them.

If you can name them, you can reach them.

By-passing the media doesn't mean trying to stiff the media. Although you may be sorely tempted to do so in contentious situations, that's asking for trouble. You want to be open, candid, and accessible to the media as a matter of policy. But don't get caught in the trap of thinking that if the media doesn't tell your story it can't be told – or if they tell it wrong it can't be corrected. Do it yourself. Go direct.

Just as all winning politics is local, all effective communications is personal.

You not only can do it personal now, you must.

Chapter Twenty One

REPUTATION MANAGEMENT

Performance alone almost never speaks for itself.

Cutting to the quick of it, all your company really has to sell is its reputation.

The CEO is the guardian of that reputation. His job is to protect it and enhance it, that is, to make it stronger. This may be his most important responsibility.

Most CEOs don't spend much time thinking about this until a crisis flares, at which juncture it is often too late.

Part of the problem is laziness...or to be more charitable, a kind of benign neglect. "Everyone knows our products are the finest and our service the best (or at least as good as any of our competitors). They know we deal fairly with them and with our employees and fix problems and are responsible in our communities. They know they can trust us and that we'll treat them right. Right!"

There is also a certain amount of righteous arrogance at play here. "We're GE (or Nordstrom or GM or any name you care to substitute) for chrissake! Everyone knows we've got the right stuff."

Either attitude leads to the conclusion that the company can more or less coast along and its reputation will take care of itself.

Wrong.

A reputation is a fragile thing. It requires constant attention.

People buy your products because of your reputation. The best and the brightest come to work for you because of your reputation. Those who invest in your stock or provide capital or permit you to operate in their communities, those who give you their loyalty and their support – do so because of your reputation.

Or they don't…because of your reputation.

Nothing ought be higher on the CEOs agenda than reputation management.

What does that mean? It means that enhancement of the firm's reputation can't be shackled by the misconception that the firm's accomplishments will speak for themselves.

Performance alone almost never speaks for itself. Performance is the cornerstone, the basic building block of reputation, but it's not enough by itself, especially when the going gets tough or when dealers or middlemen don't live up to your standards.

There may have been a time when performance alone was enough—but not anymore. The world moves too fast, there's too much clutter, too much noise, too much going on for the good performance and right actions of a single company to rise in any meaningful way above the babel of the marketplace to make its mark…*without a concentrated effort to make it happen.*

If you want your story told, you have to tell it yourself. If you want attention given to your accomplishments, you have to draw attention to them. If you want your performance known, you have to make people aware of it.

You have to manage the marketing of your reputation.

To my knowledge, a reputation management function as such doesn't exist in corporate America. Various parts of the day to day responsibility are shared out to the various line and staff operations, but there is little or no central coordination and planning – no real focus. About the only person thinking about the matter in any organized way is the Chief Public Relations Officer. And perhaps the chief marketing officer, who thinks in terms of "branding" rather than reputation. Which is all right, except that branding is seen as a commercial exercise concentrated exclusively on selling product—a one way value. Reputation, on the other hand, suggests character, caring, responsible action—a two way relationship of the firm with its constituents creating inter-relationships and mutual benefits.

Semantics aside, the compelling fact is that a company's reputation is its brand and its brand is its reputation. And the overall and inescapable responsibility for both lies with the CEO.

Though the CEO cannot shed that responsibility, he can find a trusted player to share it with him and look after it for him on a day to day basis – a senior executive who reports directly to the

CEO and who has the responsibility – and the authority – for the management of the company's reputation. A big job. An arrestingly important job. The kind of job that would go to a person whose credentials inside the company are excellent, whose commitment to the vision and ethic of the firm is complete, and whose abilities to build consensus and create buy-in are quite advanced. And, oh yes, someone who has the absolute trust of the CEO and at least the grudging respect of the overall management team. If the CPRO is any good, he should possess most of those attributes.

Unfortunately, a good reputation once won isn't permanent. It is at risk every hour of every day by every action taken by all the company's people everywhere. Which is why reputation has to be managed. The responsible CEO, through delegation or directly, makes sure all those people have the right criteria and that they are being managed to standards appropriate to the reputation he values. This can be done in an organized way through a reputation management function, or as a shared responsibility with no formal organization. The latter seems to me unnecessarily casual for the rigors to be faced in the coming decade, but whichever approach is taken, applying the company's values and ethic to the opportunities and problems that present themselves, and demonstrating the worth of those values through performance, is a dominant characteristic of successful companies.

Almost nothing of consequence happens by chance. You, of all people, know that you get what you manage for.

Chapter Twenty Two

NO SECOND CHANCES

Crisis management and damage control.

No one manages crises. When a crisis is up and running, it's too late to be managed. At that point, all that can be done is damage control. The only time a crisis can be "managed" is before it begins.

Gurus and think-tanks notwithstanding, there is nothing very complicated about crisis management or, for that matter, damage control.

Hard? Yes.

Painful? Very.

Frustrating and maddening and inordinately time consuming? Definitely.

But complicated? No.

All that's needed are guts, common sense, an interest in fair play, and honesty.

Crises come in two basic packages. They are either of the "Suprise" variety, or the "Disaster Waiting to Happen" type.

The "Suprise" variety includes acts of God (earthquake, fire, flood, hurricane) or any of the many accidental calamities that can beset an organization regardless of how well managed and responsible it may be – things like chemical spills or plant explosions.

The "Disasters Waiting To Happen" type of crisis is a different story. Largely self inflicted, this type explodes from dumb management decisions, product deficiencies, or outrage from consumers or shareholders or government and regulatory agencies over what the company has either done or failed to do. The Exxon Valdez and the Union Carbide Bophal incidents fall into this category, as do the Od-Walla recall, the Intel chip, and the AT&T downsizing crises. In fact, most of the crises which cause the most damage fall into this category. The ironic thing is, these ought to be the most manageable. The company ought to be able to see these problems coming. If they can be seen, they can be planned for. And if they can be planned for, they can be managed so as not to become a crisis.

The tragedy in these situations is that almost certainly someone somewhere in the organization knows that a condition exists or is developing that can ignite a crisis. The attorneys, the CFO, a division or unit manager, the HR head—somewhere someone knows. The crime against the organization occurs when that someone decides to keep the information to himself — to keep it secret in hopes the problem will go away, or be ignored, or not found out. When that happens, situations which might have been handle-able with the proper planning and forethought do indeed become crises.

Most often this occurs when a certain level of management misreads what senior management wants, doesn't understand what the public reaction is likely to be, or worse, is indifferent to the public reaction.

If management misreads what the public reaction is likely to be, then their public relations people aren't doing their job – assuming they've been informed and have had the chance to advise. If management is indifferent to what the public reaction will be or thinks that public reaction doesn't matter, they deserve all the hits they're going to get. If managers misread what the company expects of them and misinterpret the rules the company expects the game to be played by, then you have a problem that far exceeds any current crisis.

That said, what do you need to know about the fundamentals of crisis management and damage control to be sure you've got the right team in place and the right actions underway?

First understand that no two crises are the same, and therefore, no formulaic response can work. Crises may have similarities, but it is the differences that kill you.

While no two crises are alike, there are fundamental principles that apply in all damage control cases. These can save you. Remember, crisis management is done before the fact. Once a crisis is up and running, you're doing damage control.

Here are the principles:

Be ready. You should assume that anything that can go wrong will go wrong and have a special team in place that's ready and waiting to handle whatever may be out there. I'll come back to this.

Get the facts. Sometimes the most difficult task of all is to ferret out what the problem really is. To deal effectively with a crisis, you must know: (1) what happened; (2) why it happened; (3) what is presently being done about it; and (4) what your options are. People won't always want to be candid about what happened or why it happened. The facts might reflect badly on them. Sometimes they won't want to detail all the options. Some may be more painful than they want to bear. You, though, must have it all, and in your own self interest and that of the firm, you must be relentless in getting the information you need.

Take control of the information flow. In a fluid situation, rumors and misinformation can drown the substantive stuff and put you so far behind you never catch up. Centralize the collection and dissemination of all the information. Designate a spokesman with the exclusive authority to release information and make comments. No one else. Only him. Make sure the spokesman is well briefed and has the current information. Make sure he's always, and I mean always, available to the media. Make sure the media know who the spokesman is, how he can be reached, and understand that he's the official (and best) source for information. Underscore that the spokesman's job is to insure that the media has all the pertinent information as rapidly as it is available. Give the spokesman the absolute authority to get the information needed for truthful and timely responses.

Take the initiative. Don't wait for media queries. Get the story out yourself as fast as you can. If you tell it first you have an excellent chance of getting it told right, without undue speculation, misapprehension, or misinformation.

Tell what you know when you know it. Don't wait to get every detail. Events move too rapidly. If you miss the chance to make your points because you don't have all the information ready right then, the chance may be missed forever. Don't worry about information changing. Have your people take the position that "This is what we know now. Later information may supercede it. If it does, we'll get to you right away."

Get all the bad news out as rapidly as possible. Don't string it out. A running story puts you at risk of dying the death of a thousand cuts.

Tell it straight. Don't let your spokesman dance around or try fancy footwork. Don't ask him to dissemble or try to sugar-coat the facts. Tell it like it is.

Let people know as rapidly, and as widely, as possible what steps are being taken to fix the problem. And keep telling them. Don't assume that a point once made has registered, or that everyone who should have heard has heard.

Take the story directly to your constituents. By this I mean directly to the people who are affected by the problem and the people whose actions or opinions can help or hurt you. Don't rely on the media to carry your message for you. Take it directly to them, in your words, using some of the tools discussed earlier, and keep on doing this through the run of the exercise.

Try to do what's right. This is the key to any damage control situation. If you are really trying to do what's right and responsible and fair, you'll get the benefit of the doubt and you'll get support. Unfortunately, what the public thinks is right and what the company is prepared to do aren't always the same. In which case you have a much bigger problem.

The Golden Rule of crisis management and damage control is this: prevent the crisis. This step takes place before the act – not after. It is a matter of fully understanding the consequences of what the company is planning to do and taking the necessary steps to make those actions responsible and understandable to your constituents.

To achieve this, you need a specific team paying attention to the probable consequences of the company's various actions and prepared to manage whatever reactions might come. Call this anything you like – the Issues Team, the Alpha Team, the X Committee. Whatever it's called, all organizations of any consequence should have such a team and it ought to be working on a regular basis in an active oversight capacity for the entire organization. The team needs full authority to get answers and take action. It should be as small as possible, but with a core group composed of the chief public relations officer, the chief marketing officer, the chief financial officer, the chief counsel, the chief human resources officer, and the chief operating officer. Subject matter experts can be brought in and out depending on the nature of the challenge. This group ought to meet at least monthly. Its purpose is to scan the terrain for landmines and defuse them before they can explode. This requires constant vigilance, not a casual glance every now and then. When it misses a landmine and a crisis blows up, the group will meet daily, sometimes several times a day, to evaluate information, decide the course of action in consultation with the CEO, and monitor the corrective steps.

Classic damage control theory says find out what your constituents want you to do to fix the problem and do it! If that's not going to happen, if your organization isn't prepared to do what your constituents think is right and fair—or cannot do so for reasons of cost, or available technology, or whatever—then all you can do is try to keep the crisis contained and make your case as best you can *directly* to your most important constituents.

Even if they don't like it, if you can get them to understand why you are convinced you must do what has been done, then you have a reasonable chance of saving a long term relationship. Notice the emphasis on the word "directly." While the media is enormously important in damage control situations, getting your message to your key constituents is too critical to be left to others in hopes they will do it for you. Use the all the tools available to take it direct.

Also note the phrase "key constituents." They're the same people we discussed in Chapter Twenty on going direct. While we'd all like it very much, it isn't possible to be known and loved by all. And it isn't necessary. But it is absolutely imperative that the people and groups whose opinion and actions can help you or hurt you understand the rationale for your actions and believe that you do what you do because you're convinced it is the right course for your organization. These people, those who can help or hurt, are your key constituents. If they believe you're trying to do the right thing, or at the very least are not being driven by wanton disregard for the public weal, you may come out okay.

One final point: play the CEO card thoughtfully.

In the early stages of damage control exercises of any real consequence, there may be a fair amount of pressure for the CEO to step out in front and take the lead. This is fairly standard procedure. A crisis flares. The CEO rushes to the spot. A press conference is called. The CEO allows as how sorry the company is for whatever did or didn't happen and pledges to get the matter fixed as rapidly as possible and make sure it never happens again.

Great stuff. It shows that the company is responsive, responsible, and sensitive. If the CEO is involved, clearly the company takes the matter seriously. If the CEO puts his authority behind getting the problem fixed, it will get fixed. If the CEO is willing to say he's sorry the incident occurred, it shows the company truly regrets what happened and will do what is necessary to prevent a recurrence.

All aces.

Still, as in other games of chance, timing can be everything. Cornell Maier of Kaiser Aluminum, one of the most intuitive CEOs I've ever known, had a rule about timing: never make an important decision before you have to, lest you foreclose the opportunity to make a better one. Never wait too long to make a decision or you may wind up having the decision made for you by time and events.

The CEO card is one of the strongest in your hand in crisis situations. *Never* play it just because you have it. *Always* play it when the corporation's reputation is at stake, or when public health or safety is at issue, or the environment at serious risk.

Chapter Twenty Three

COOPERATIVE CONFRONTATION

Special interests groups, activists and other stimulants.

There are four important things to understand about dealing with activists and special interest groups:

(1) They want publicity.

(2) They want respect.

(3) Fair only works one way.

(4) Working together isn't as improbable as sometimes it seems.

Special interest groups in general, and activists in particular, live off publicity. Theirs is a very competitive world. To raise funds, to attract others of a like mind, to project a persona, to be feared or respected or loved...they must be seen and known. They have to have attention. Lots of it. Propter hoc, publicity! You're familiar with the drill. Pickets, sit-ins, protests, demonstrations, accusations. Lights, camera, action! Anything for the media and don't take it personal.

When a visiting black bishop came to the headquarters city of a certain corporation at the height of the anti-apartheid struggle in South Africa, that firm was chosen as the principal target for a major demonstration. The fact that the firm was innocent of any such practices and didn't operate in South Africa was beside the point. What was relevant was that the company was the largest in town and the plaza in front of its headquarters' building was the best place in town to stage a major media event. Tag. You're it.

Once you understand that publicity might be the real object of the exercise, a number of possibilities open up.

Pacific Gas & Electric, then the country's largest investor owned utility, found that out as it got ready to bring on-line a massive nuclear powered electrical generator in Southern California. Anti-nuclear and environmental activists threatened bodily intervention to prevent the start-up. PG&E sat down to talk things out with the activist leaders. As it turned out, the activists had no real expectation of preventing the start-up. What they wanted was attention to their cause. All PG&E wanted was to get their plant on line without damage to property or personnel. So PG&E decided to see if a bargain could be struck. It could. PG&E would use its considerable resources to help the activists get all the press attention they wanted. The activists, in turn, would stage their protests without interrupting PG&E operations or putting life at risk. PG&E set up an on-site press room, helped the protesters schedule interviews and coverage, provided phone and telegraph lines back to the various news outlets.

The activists acted with civility. PG&E got its plant on-line without incident. The activists got their publicity. They called it "cooperative confrontation."

The important lesson here is that in the case of demonstrations, pickets, rallies, sit-ins, boycotts, or confrontations in general, if each side can understand the *realistic* expectations of the other, and *will talk constructively with each other,* ways can be found to accommodate both. Not always and everywhere, but often enough to make the effort worthwhile.

The sides, though, have to be willing to talk and to listen. Listening is the hard part, maybe harder than getting the process started before all the vitriol starts spewing in the media—which is a very important thing to do. If you want this to happen, you'll have to take the initiative. Whomever you've assigned to be your company's interface with, and pulse taker of, the various special interest groups that impact you, will have to find out who the other principals are and make the overtures to them. It's not always easy to know who the real leaders of these groups are. Some are in the limelight. Some are in command. There is a real problem when the two are confused.

This is how acting before the fact helps: you have a practice that is being criticized and is, perhaps, under attack. You're taking corrective steps. These steps may be seen as not substantive enough, or not fast enough; nevertheless, you're trying. Your people arrange a meeting with the leaders of your critics. No press around. No fanfare. You demonstrate that you recognize the problem. You brief them on what you're doing and on what you feel you can do to solve it. You get their reactions, their input. You open an ongoing dialogue, a let's-reason-together dialogue. You don't pretend you have the problem solved, but you do show you're working on it seriously and with a determination to reach a fair solution. And you keep talking…and listening. If you're honest and sincere, and they are too, you'll keep the event from flaming into a crisis, and you'll have a fighting chance at finding an accommodation both can live with.

This is tricky ground. Different people have different agendas. Some of your critics may truly want to find a solution. Some may want a platform from which to leap to grander things, in which case they're there to use you. Don't permit that. And you may find that fair only works one way – as in it's only fair that they get what they want. The impact on your company isn't part of the equation. You may also find that however much you're prepared to do, it isn't enough. What can possibly be enough when justice is at stake? Even so, persevere. Responsible people who really want to find solutions usually can find them. And think very, very carefully about playing the CEO card. If you become personally involved once the issue is public, the publicity values increase exponentially and your negotiating room declines similarly. Be patient.

In all cases:

Be courteous.

Don't tolerate demagoguery or threats.

Don't pontificate or make threats yourself.

Respect the other's position.

Insist that yours be respected as well.

And never let your people loose their cool.

Chapter Twenty Four

THE BYRD RULE

Working with government.

It was one of those humid summer afternoons on Capitol Hill with a thunderstorm threatening. We were in the presence of the right honorable Robert C. Byrd, senior senator from West Virginia, the state in whose rural confines we had our biggest plant and several thousand employees. We thought we were doing well. Our cause was just, our points were cogent, the senator nodded appreciatively at all the right places. Just as we were warming to the close he held up his hand and said, "Listen, fellows, you don't have to convince me. Convince my constituents. If they're for you, I'm for you. If they're against you, there isn't a way on God's green earth I'm going to support you."

That statement, as succinctly as any I've heard, sums up a primary law of lobbying. Senator Byrd's admonition also underscored the truth of that old political bromide – all politics is local.

The point of the Senator's comment became obvious quite rapidly. If we hoped to be successful with whatever initiative we wanted to lay before our elected representatives (local, county, state, or federal) we had to create an atmosphere of acceptance among his constituents *that would permit him* to make the decision or take the action we sought. We didn't have to convince him. We had to convince his constituents. He's for what they're for. We knew that, of course. We knew that anything that helps the politician get elected, or re-elected, is good. Anything that threatens same is bad. And anything that distresses constituents is something to be studiously avoided. What the people in New York or California or Ohio think doesn't make a lot of difference. What makes the difference is what the people who elect the candidate think, and getting elected is what the politician thinks about. We knew that, too. We had just never had it put so clearly before. So we went to work selling opinion-leading members of his constituency on our position. We made an effort to educate activists to neutralize opposition and spent time with editorial boards to generate media understanding. What we were working for was the situation in which, when the member said to his staff, "Check out what the folks at home think about this," he got a response that said either, "They are okay with it," or, "They don't care. It ain't on their radar screens." In which case the member had "permission" to make the decision or take the action we wanted without concern of constituency back-fire. It was a great lesson.

This doesn't mean the member will always go along with you even though his folks aren't against it. He may be trading chits with other members, or simply may not like what you want to do. But if you haven't done the groundwork, the chances you'll get what you want are fairly rare.

Most of the day-to-day and face-to-face work of governmental matters will be done by your staff, of course – the specialists who work directly for you or for the lobbying firms you've hired in Washington and the states where you operate. But as with the media, you have take an active role in establishing and maintaining contacts with the senior politicians in all your important venues. And as with the media, you'll want close relationships with a core group of senators, representatives, and governors.

This can get to be pretty heady stuff and may tempt you to become personally active in politics. Don't. The downside is far larger than any benefit you'll derive.

You'll be much more comfortable working with governmental types than with media, of course. They talk your language. They understand deals and negotiating. They're perfectly happy to operate behind closed doors and in private. You should trust none of them to any important degree. They will do whatever benefits them most, regardless of the impact on you or your company.

On the matter of money – if your PAC is making noticeable contributions to candidate X or Y, and you're generous in your participation at thousand-dollar-a-plate dinners and are giving to the limit of campaign appeals, you'll have access. Despite protestations to the contrary, access equals influence. If you want influence, you've gotta give. This is a sorry state of affairs, but it is the way the game is played. As you play, be careful. Make sure your attorneys certify that you follow every nuance of the political contributions laws. Someday, some top corporate official is going to jail for over-enthusiasm in this area. On the list of things-not-worth-going-to-jail-for, this has to be the highest.

Chapter Twenty Five

AS HEARD ON THE STREET

Where credibility is almost as important as performance.

If you're not a publicly traded company, or don't expect to be one day, you can skip this (although several of the points are worth noting as guides to corporate conduct in general).

The first reality of investor relations is that if you want to make it on The Street, you have to be believed. That means you have to be able to deliver on whatever expectations you've created or that you've allowed to form in the minds of others (particularly security analysts) by what you've said, inferred, or permitted to be perceived. Nowhere in your universe is the management of expectations more important than in dealing with your investor constituency, and nowhere is more attention required to keep the balance right.

Tom Clausen of Bank of America had a wonderful rule for handling this conundrum. "Under promise, over perform," he'd tell his people. Clausen used the rule masterfully in the dark days when it looked as if Bank of America was on its last legs and even more skillfully as the bank made its remarkable turn-around.

Managing the up-side expectations takes real discipline. Managing the down-side expectations takes real talent. We should all have confidence in our potential and enthusiasm for our prospects. But let the market expect more than we're going to be able to deliver and we're in big trouble. Let the market seriously underestimate our potential, though, and we've robbed our shareholders of value. Tough balancing feat to achieve.

Keeping the balance right is the job of your Investor Relations people – and you. The only tool you have for this is communication – regular, candid, responsible communications to your share-holders, to the security analysts who follow you, to the rating agencies who judge you, and to the regulators who watch you.

As with media relations, this is something you can't be divorced from. You have to monitor the activity to be sure it's up to your standards of responsible disclosure (which hopefully exceed the minimum disclosures required by law) and you have to be a participant. The key shareholders and key analysts, in particular, need regular contact with you—face-to-face, by phone, or by written message—but regular and substantive contact. And you need to play an active role in determining what messages are to be delivered and in what detail.

Security analysts are a punishing lot. It's nothing personal, but mislead them with rosy projections, or allow them to be misled by silence or sleight-of-hand, and you'll find yourself in very short order rewriting that old observation about what hell hath no fury like.

It takes a little longer with shareholders, but the same result occurs. As it does with the rating agencies and the regulators.

The manager of a major fund put it this way. "Once credibility has been destroyed, the company's stock is going to keep moving down and nothing can be done unless the company can collateralize its promises."

Perhaps more to the point is the observation of a ranking security analyst. "Once a company's credibility has been destroyed, the company will keep sinking until the CEO walks the plank."

On Wall Street, credibility is almost as important as performance. Communicate. Candidly.

Chapter Twenty Six

PUBLIC OPINION DON'T COUNT

Actionable opinion is all that matters.

There is no such thing as public opinion anymore. Maybe there never was. Maybe there was only the assumed consensus of the white, English speaking, establishment majority in the days when there were only three national newsmagazines, three national television networks, three national newswire services, and no national newspaper to speak of. Maybe, when the channels for the distribution of news and opinion were so few and when those few seemed to be singing off the same hymnal on this issue or that, maybe the opinion of the majority in this country did coalesce into something that could be assumed to represent the attitudes of most of the public.

But no more. The Balkanization of the media, the fragmentation of the society into ethnic and national groups insisting on a special separateness, and the dissolution of shared values, makes the notion that the majority of people in this country will hold similar opinions on issues of substance a bit hard to swallow...anymore. Shared opinions rise from shared values and shared experiences.

What does exist, and what is of tremendous importance to you, are the opinions held by your constituents.

So my brief here is to convince you that you shouldn't be very much concerned with "public opinion" to the extent anyone applies that label to attitudes about your operation – but that you must be mightily concerned about constituent opinion.

You and your administration stand for election every day. Your constituents are the usual suspects—your shareholders, your customers, your employees, the communities in which you work, the government representatives in whose jurisdictions you do business. These forces vote for or against you almost hourly in the way they interact with you. They buy your products. Or don't. They give you a good day's work. Or don't. They help you with a good business environment. Or don't. Without their votes, you're out. These are the people whose opinions and actions can help you the most. Or hurt you the most. And it is on them that your attention should be focused.

And one turn further. Your attention should be focused on *actionable public opinion*. Pollsters will tell you that people are perfectly happy to offer opinions about almost anything – even things they don't have an opinion on. This has something to do with wanting to please the pollster, or not appearing dumb. People even hold opinions, strong opinions, about matters which they will never take a step to advance.

The only opinions that make a difference, then, are the opinions held by your constituents upon which they are likely to act— actionable public opinion. Everything else is just smoke and mirrors.

The trick is to know what's actionable and what's not. Good research can tell you. It needn't be expensive. All that feel good stuff about in what high esteem you're held by the public, or where you rank against your competitors, or whether on a scale of one to ten they'd rate your stock a good purchase is interesting and may even be useful. But what counts is what the people who can help you the most or hurt you the most think—*and are likely to do*—about the things you're doing or want to do.

To find this out, if you don't already have one, get a sharp, preferably small, polling organization, ideally one with some experience in political polling. Do not use a marketing research group or the arm of your advertising or PR agency. You want street-smart pros who have mastered the art of identifying actionable public opinion and who can give you good answers rapidly. Have them produce regular read-outs. A pulse-taking every now and then, or once yearly check up, isn't frequent enough. Do it monthly. Daily if you're in trouble or in the midst of a high visibility activity. (This is one of the best crisis management tools you can employ – remembering that crisis management means avoiding land-mines.)

Focus the pollsters on the issues and initiatives important to your goals. Use the intelligence they provide to plan or modify your strategies. Don't guess about these matters, or let anecdotal information mislead you into thinking you know all you need to know. Like Senator Byrd, if your constituents aren't with you, you can't win. And how can they be with you if you don't meet their wants and needs? And how can you do that if you don't know what those wants and needs are?

Having said all this good stuff about research, let me raise a caution. Be a healthy skeptic about research results. Research can be shaped to produce almost any answer you want. Make sure your people aren't feeding you what they think you want to hear – or equally as bad, what, for purposes of their own, they want you to hear. Bad intelligence loses wars.

Chapter Twenty Seven

A MATTER OF STYLE

The CEO's persona.

One of the consequences of becoming CEO is that you lose your public anonymity. On the way to the top some very important people will have known who you are, of course, but there will not have been a lot of them and for the most part they will have been inside the company. Now shareholders will know you, and all of your employees. The media will know you, and customers and suppliers and leaders of the companies in your competitive universe. Heads of charitable foundations, deans of business schools, influentials in government and politics, civic improvement groups, directors of other companies on whose boards you'll be invited to sit – you won't be largely anonymous anymore. You'll have power. You will be of consequence.

Another result of moving into the CEO chair is that you take on a new set of responsibilities and expectations. Not just responsibility for running the business. It's not as simple as that. All those constituents out there will now look to you as the new leader, the problem solver, the maker of miracles.

With so much attention on you, you've got to give serious consideration to how you want to be seen and thought of by all these folks. How they see and think of you can have a major impact on your success and the success of your firm.

I know CEOs are innately modest, unassuming men who just want to be let alone to do the job they were hired to do, thank you kindly, ma'am – without fanfare, adulation, or undue notice. The idea of intentionally setting out to project a persona, to establish a positioning which differentiates you in a special way, may seem immodest at best.

It isn't. It is necessary.

Every leader has some special attribute or set of attributes that attracts others to him, gives them confidence, makes them willing to follow. Consider the style of Jack Welch, Lee Iacocca, Chuck Schwab, Dave Packard – the kind of leaders men storm barricades for and shareholders love. Examine your attributes. They make the fabric of your persona. Build on them. Analyze your strengths. Project them. Do this consistently and in self-reinforcing ways through your manner and your actions. Smart, tough, thoughtful, articulate, aggressive, innovative, a winner – whatever set of attributes you truly possess should be assembled, polished, packaged, and marketed to help build the trust and support you need to achieve your objectives.

This takes analysis and planning. Analysis first by you and your closest associates who understand the drill and whose opinions you respect. Then planning by your CPRO with you to find channels through which the persona can be projected and the positioning achieved in a natural way.

Calculating? Perhaps, but taking steps to project the right persona, to establish the right positioning, is part of your responsibility to your shareholders and your employees. You are the leader of the team. You set the tone and the character of the organization. You are the public personification of the corporation, the keeper of the flame and the protector of its reputation. What people think of you, the way they see you, will in large measure determine their attitudes toward the corporation on your watch. If you don't take the steps necessary to maximize your value to the firm, you do a disservice to yourself and to your shareholders – modesty and humility notwithstanding.

There are, of course, risks here. The persona has to be built on an honest assessment of who you are and what you stand for. Anything phony will be found out and you'll be crucified.

The positioning must be established on a candid appraisal of how you stand out from your competitors. You may be surprised when you look at this objectively.

Your critics, inside the company and out, may accuse you of ego tripping or worse if the thrust of the exercise becomes obvious (which it shouldn't). Ignore them. Little minds have little impact.

Don't side-step this matter out of modesty or concerns for privacy. The CEO is a major company asset to be deployed in ways that serve the company's interest.

Chapter Twenty Eight

THE CEO'S COMMUNICATIONS

Building consent and consensus.

Few things you do as CEO will be more important than what you communicate and the way in which you do it. Communication is the quintessential management skill. If you can't communicate effectively, you can't manage effectively.

You communicate in many ways – the expression on your face, the body language you show, the gestures you make. You communicate by your choice of words, by the way you speak and write, and through actions you take or don't take. The only way you reach others—to get their help, their advice, their participation and their support—is through communications. Every thing you do communicates.

You probably think you're pretty good at this already. Maybe you are. But you've got to be better. Your predecessors could manage by command and control. They told people what to do and how to do it and took names and kicked butt to make it happen in fairly rigid, hierarchical style organizations. Your management generation can't do that. The rules and the relationships have changed too much. People won't stand still for the authoritarian way anymore. They want to understand what's happening and be a part of the process. You have to manage by consent and consensus—by building teams, encouraging innovation, pointing the way, and shepherding everyone to goals they've bought in to. Building consent and consensus requires masterful communications. You don't have to be a Ronald Reagan or a Jack Welch, but you do have to:

▪ Treat the people who work for and with you like adults who deserve to know how the business is doing, what its opportunities and problems are, what's needed from them, and what they can expect from you. Not every now and then, but regularly. And set up information channels to make it happen.

▪ Dismantle the need-to-know mentality that handcuffs every attempt at successful internal communications and replace it with a share-the-information mind-set. From shared information come new ideas and better solutions, which lead of course, to heightened competitiveness and greater successes in the marketplace.

▪ You have to be honest and candid with all those inside and outside the corporation whose interests are in any way affected by the firm's actions and plans. You tell it first. You tell it straight. And you tell it as thoroughly as laws, regulations, and competitive conditions permit.

▪ And you need a voice—a distinctive manner in both your spoken and written communications that is unmistakably yours. Some are more skillful at projecting this than others. If you're not among the most skillful, get help. Get one or two "articulators" to help you phrase your ideas clearly and persuasively. Use them regularly. Your CPRO, one of your senior management colleagues whose opinions you value and whose discretion you trust, a very good outside writer—these make a good team. Most of what people know about you will come from what they read, or from what they hear you say, or from what others say they heard you say. In whatever way you're perceived, you want to be as articulate and thoughtful as possible.

Much of your most effective communication will be person to person – in the form of presentations to customer, employee, or shareholder groups; video interviews and reports; major speeches to significant business and public groups; at the shareholders' meeting, etc. Most managers are terrible performers in these venues. They come across as apprehensive, nervous, squeaky-voiced, grim-faced, and awful. Or worse, they think they're super and don't do the preparation. They throw away the carefully crafted script and take off to wing-it to the boredom of the audience.

For your person to person communications, get help also. Even if you're good at it. There are excellent trainers who, in one or two sessions, can give you the polish and presence and delivery style you need to come across with impact before any audience. If you're good already, a trainer will make you better. Find one. Use him. Prepare with him. Rehearse with him. Critique with him.

When you're in the field, take a lesson from the politicians and press the flesh. Don't spend all your time with the local managers and customers, get out and meet the people who do the day to day work, shake hands, ask how they're doing, find out what's on their minds.

Once a month, or once a quarter, have lunch with the troops. Have your personnel department, in coordination with the line and staff units, select six to twelve high performers and invite them to a special lunch with you (at corporate headquarters for those close by, and in the field when you're traveling). Make it informal. Spend time getting to know each other over lunch. Afterwards, take twenty minutes or so. Tell them how much you appreciate their work, discuss the current state of the business, or if there is a particular problem or opportunity or your mind, talk it over with them. Then invite them to tell you what's on their mind. The positive word of mouth about these sessions feeding back through the grape-vine is money in the bank. And the things you learn in this unfiltered, unstructured atmosphere are invaluable.

Finally in this regard, if you can get comfortable with the camera, make video your medium of choice for employee communications when you can't do it face to face. You still need print – memos, newsletters, etc. Nothing beats print for relaying information. But for emotion, there is no equal to TV. And much of what you need to communicate – your vision, your enthusiasm, your leadership – is a matter of emotion.

Even if the CEO isn't the best communicator in the organization, his *communications* can be the best. All it takes is determination.

Chapter Twenty Nine

THE MOST IMPORTANT CONSTITUENCY

Not the conventional wisdom.

Poll any group of CEOs of publicly held companies as to their most important constituency and the answer will overwhelmingly be their shareholders.

The logic goes something like this: We work for the shareholders. Our job is to increase shareholder value. Shareholders are our *raison d'être*. Our most important constituency, clearly, is our shareholders.

Don't subscribe to this fiction.

An organization's most important constituency is its employees. This has always been the case and will be true in spades in the new century.

For the fact and truth of the matter is that if your employees aren't with you and for you, nothing of any consequence happens. Quality products don't get made or competitive products marketed. The company's bottom line suffers and shareholders' interests aren't served.

Employees are the most important constituency. So pay careful attention to them. They'll make the difference for you in the new millenium.

In fact, your single biggest ongoing challenge may well be your ability to attract, retain, and motivate a quality work force. The difference between being a winner and an also-ran will be the quality of the team you're able to field against your competition.

Personnel consultants and management gurus will make a large fortune out of helping you deal with this challenge in the years ahead. They'll earn it. In the meantime, a few thoughts to keep in mind:

- It is a remarkable thing, but people really do have a tendency to act as they are treated. Which is to say, respect begets respect, trust begets trust, enthusiasm begets enthusiasm. Provide a work atmosphere that offers these, plus an environment that encourages people to see just how far their grasp can extend and you'll have a reasonable chance at being competitive.

- Despite what the old research shows about the importance of job satisfaction, money is a key motivator and since people can't count on job security as they could in the dear departed past, it will be an even bigger motivator in the future. So to get and keep good people, be prepared to pay for the privilege.

- Put away the command and control mentality and retire the hierarchical managers. Work on consent and consensus.

Chapter Thirty

BUY-IN

Without it you can't succeed.

There have been a lot of references to buy-in in this tome.

Up until the time of the great greed-and-take-no-prisoners phase that began in the early 80's, your predecessor managers didn't have to worry much about buy-in. They were still in the command and control mode. Employees generally signed on for the duration and more or less trusted the company to look out for them. Investors were more passive. The media was a little less prosecutorial. The world, overall, seemed a more benign place.

Benign isn't an adjective that applies to the world of the new century. Employees will be far less trusting, investors far more demanding, the media far more intrusive, and your world overall far more ominous. To make it in this world, you have to be able to create buy-in.

Buy-in is that happy state when the people who are important to the success of your initiatives understand what you want to do. They approve of it. They support it. They actively participate in ways that are appropriate to help you reach your goals (or at the very least don't put impediments in your path). They're on your side because you've shown them your vision and helped them see the good things that can happen for them if they are a part of it. And they like what they see.

The key to creating buy-in is your ability to understand the wants and needs of your constituents and find ways to associate their interests with your actions. The strongest single tool for achieving this is communications.

The conceits that work against buy-in are:
- arrogance

- ignorance
- disrespect
- greed
- dishonesty
- and insensitivity.

The attributes that work for buy-in are:
- openness
- candor
- responsiveness
- accessibility
- empathy
- and fairness.

The deciding factor in creating buy-in is *you*. If you are of the stuff in which people can believe, if you can show them a future they find desirable and convince them you can lead them there – if you can do these things you'll have your buy-in.

Chapter Thirty One

WHAT'S IN A NAME

A brief overview of pr.

In most organizations, the function with the portfolio for helping the CEO create and sustain buy-in, for shepherding the reputation management function, and handling the crises, and keeping the baying media at large, and a host of other assignments, is called Public Relations. Or Public Affairs. Or Corporate Communications. One of the curious aspects of the function is that the people who do it can't agree on what to call it. As a result of this ambiguity, most executives in most organizations have only the foggiest idea of what the tool can do and, consequently, very little idea of how to use it effectively.

It's time to find out.

Whatever name it's given (for the purposes of this discussion let's call it Public Relations) the function isn't about affairs or relating or communicating. It is about getting people to do something, not do something, or let you do something. This bears repeating. *The function is about getting people to do something, not do something, or let you do something.* It is about getting people to buy your products, buoy your stock price, be good employees, let you build that plant or make that acquisition, not oppose your legislative interests. The function is about affecting behavior and is a serious management tool that can do what no other single tool can do when properly used.

The Public Relations function in almost all companies have certain qualities in common. These include an expertise in mass and interpersonal communications, in media relations, in governmental affairs, and in investor relations. There usually is a corps of creative people constantly looking for new ways to draw attention to and sustain interest in products and services and to phrase, package, and deliver ideas that advance the corporation's interests. Experts in crisis management and damage control and in community relations and employee communications usually are part of the group as well.

These are the seven unique ways the tool helps you reach your goals:

1. It creates support and builds a sense of team among employees by helping them understand what you're trying to achieve and how they benefit from helping the company reach its goals. (Internal Communications)

2. It creates interest in the strengths of the business and an appreciation for its prospects which support the stock price and overall financing efforts. (Investor Relations and Financial Communications)

3. It fashions an atmosphere of public understanding around issues and actions which allow law makers and regulators to be supportive of the organization and it develops and manages the persuasive presentation of the organization's case to key lawmakers and regulators. (Governmental Relations)

4. It draws attention to and creates interest in the corporation's products and services in direct support of the marketing effort. (Marketing Communications and Product Publicity)*

5. It identifies potential problems before they explode and either defuses them or lays strategies to minimize their impact. (Crisis Management)

6. If a crisis is up and running, it takes the actions necessary to put the problem down. (Damage Control)

7. And it provides the interface with the media that generates reasonable attention to the company's achievements and a fair hearing in times of trouble. (Media Relations)

This isn't an exhaustive list of the function's scope. Responsibilities such as corporate advertising, corporate philanthropy, opinion research, etc., are often part of the portfolio. But these are the core disciplines.

*A Footnote Regarding Marketing Communications

A trend is developing as we move into the new millenium to meld the marketing communications function of the Public Relations Department into a broader effort called Integrated Marketing. The idea is to reap the considerable synergistic and cost benefits that ought to accrue from integrating, coordinating, and controlling all the functions the company uses to reach its customers in one place and under one management. This is a fine objective. But it can carry with it a danger you want to avoid. That danger is the conclusion that Public Relations is a marketing function.

It isn't.

Public Relations is a CEO function. Correctly staffed and rightly managed, it is the only function in the organization, outside the CEO's office, with the experience and credentials to attend to the broad agenda of the corporation in its interactions with all its constituencies. No tunnel vision. No one constituency focus. No blinders. It is obligated to see the corporation clearly, to understand its goals, to know the expectations and wants of its constituencies, and to use the talents and experience at its disposal to help the individual business units reach their goals, and you reach yours.

Marketing communications is one of the things a good PR operation can do well, but PR is not one of the things a good marketing operation can do well. The talents and mind-sets of the people, their skills and experiences, their values and their drives, are too different. CEOs who have assumed otherwise have come to considerable distress when the chips are down and gut corporate issues are on the line and they find themselves with only marketing minded people with marketing experience to rely on. If the Integrated Marketing approach appeals, and there is much in its favor, make PR a partner, but not a captive. And reserve to the Chief Public Relations officer full oversight authority for the company's core interests.

That understood, the challenge then becomes one of using the complete tool effectively...of making it an integral part of each year's operating plan at both the tactical and strategic level and using its multiple implements separately and in combination to achieve the results you seek.

The function should report to the CEO. The act of deciding how the organization should present itself, and with what voice, and to whom, is too important a matter to be outside the CEO's personal control, so the reporting line should be direct, with no gatekeepers in between. The CEO is the corporation's de facto public relations chief. He may delegate the day to day management of the function, but the buck stops with him. It is the CEO who personifies the organization's values, the CEO who articulates the vision, the CEO who sets the objectives, and increasingly the CEO who takes the rap when things don't work out as well as constituents hoped. Given what he has at stake, then, it is the CEO who ought to have the most concern about how the organization is presented to its key constituents. He ought to care very much about how its reputation is maintained, how its progress is described, how its problems are explained, and how its potential is projected – care enough to be personally involved.

To get the most mileage out of the effort, the functional portfolio ought to include: reputation management, employee communications, media relations, financial communications and investor relations, public information and education, governmental relations, contributions, marketing communications and product publicity, corporate advertising, issues management, and crisis management and damage control.

Some companies do group the connected functions in this manner. In companies that don't, it is more a matter of practice and tradition than a practical analysis of organizational effectiveness. All these functions are discrete parts of a larger whole. They share disciplines, skills, and mind-sets. Put them together and a remarkably effective tool is at hand.

As for budgets, the dollars needed to run a good operation are quite low in comparison to other expenses. On average and excluding advertising, budgets representing one quarter to one half of one percent of sales seem to work for many *Fortune 500* companies. In the context of most corporate budgets, small potatoes.

A first rate staff is needed to run all this—real pros with experience and cajones. If you have such a staff count yourself lucky. If you don't, start building. Staff size need not be overly large, just sufficient. Among the *Fortune 500*, staffs range from as few as four to as many as several hundred—depending on the components of their portfolios and the geographic reach of the company.

Some companies, big companies, intentionally keep the in-house staff small – four or five of the best people they can find – and use outsourcing to provide the rest of what's needed. This is one of the areas in which outsourcing works extremely well—as long as there is a strong internal cadre to keep things focused. Other companies like to do it all themselves with their own people. They think they get a better result.

There is no rule here, just an admonition: Know what the tool is for, and use it aggressively.

Chapter Thirty Two

A FEW LIKELY DEVELOPMENTS

No place for the meek and no time for fancy footwork.

One of the defining characteristics of the world of the new millenium will be instantaneous information on everything from everywhere—all the time. Hyped by the Internet, and around the clock radio and TV news, and broadcast newsmagazines and talk shows offering a wide range of foolishness ad infinitum, everything reportable will be reported, along with a lot that's not.

The downside implications of all this are enormous. The voracious demand of the media for material to fill its gluttonous craw will result in a steady deterioration of news values and news standards. More sobering, it will cause an erosion in the quality of the people who gather and decide what the public will see and hear— for the simple reason that there won't be enough good people to go around. Demand for really good people already exceeds the supply. By the early years of the next decade much of the media product will be coming from a swarm of mediocre people with mediocre credentials scrambling to be first with the worst. The dean of a well respected school of communications at a major university summarized the situation this way. "Until we start turning out people who can recognize the difference between a wild assertion and a verifiable fact – and care enough to respect the distinction – we're all in trouble."

And that's a real problem because it means the job of getting a fair and responsible shake from a large portion of the media may become increasingly more difficult as the new millenium unfolds. Which is why your attention to the key five media and your ability to identify and go directly to your key constituents is so important.

One of the consequences of dealing with a deteriorating media situation is that business organizations will increasingly take the initiative to get the bad news out first. This will be a positive development. Institutions will come to understand that if bad news is "discovered" by a media outlet, the outlet defines the problem. That definition may be totally foreign to the institution's perception of reality or, at best, a set of confused and unnecessarily harmful assumptions that once broadcast publicly may be impossible to correct. The institution is then forced into trying to explain the negatives – a no win situation. So you will increasingly take the initiative in bad news situations.

You will do this partly because the rushing trend to judgmental journalism will continue pell mell. Judgmental journalism is that situation in which editors and writers pass judgement on the subject before the reportage begins. Competition forces much of this—the need to out-shout or out-sensationalize the competition, to get attention, to deliver readers and viewers by seducing them away from others. This isn't going to abate in the new century.

Another result is that you and your colleagues, concerned that the odds of getting fair reportage from responsible journalists are shrinking, will increasingly by-pass the media and take your story directly to your constituents as we discussed in Chapter Twenty.

You'll also be involved in a rising level of corporate candor. There really is such a thing as "the public's right to know"—not codified anywhere but firmly ingrained in our democratic traditions. People do have a right to know about those things which affect their jobs, their safety, their health, their investments, and the quality of life in the communities in which they live. They have a right to know about these things in sufficient detail and in sufficient time to permit them to take whatever actions they feel are in their best interests. Most companies act as if service of the public's right to know is the exclusive franchise of the media. That's a mistake. You have as much right and as much responsibility to serve that "right" as does the media and you ought to exercise it in your own self interest.

So candor will come to be the norm.

One of the nice things about candor is that it is so disarming.

Along with candor, the smart companies will become more assertive. In some circles this might be considered contentious, but it need not be. Any time there is substantial misreportage, intentional or not, malicious or not, damaging or not, it should be corrected. The media record stands for all time, and errors once on the record, if not corrected, keep getting repeated and soon become part of the revealed wisdom. It's not necessary to pick a fight to get the record corrected. Most responsible media people want to be right and will correct errors if asked to do so. Still, occasions from time to time arise when the error is so blatant or the misreportage so bruising that a little confrontation may be necessary. That's OK. Despite the conventional wisdom about picking fights with people who buy their ink by the barrel, you can take on the media, and you can win—if you're right. General Motors and Food Lion and Kaiser Aluminum proved that.

Actually, media and business ought to have a similar objective in the matter of the public information. Clearly the two work from different frames of reference and carry different charters, but the shared responsibility—and objective—ought to be to see to it that the publics involved have the information they need in order to make informed judgments in their own best interests. Where most of the difficulties arise is in agreeing on what, when, and how much information is sufficient.

Regardless of the mutual frustration often felt by both, in the pursuit of an informed public, business ought to be able to expect objectivity, fairness, substance, and balance from the media. And demand it when it's not there.

Similarly, from business the media ought to be able to expect honesty, openness, candor, and accessibility. And demand it when it's not there.

Will this happy state ever arrive? Probably not. The relationship between business and the media, while truly symbiotic, has an inescapable adversarial core when issues of substance are on the line. There's nothing wrong with that. The public interest is probably best served because of it. Even so, both business and the media ought not lose sight of what the public has a right to expect from both, and ought try to manage their relationship with responsibility, intelligence, good humor, and grace. Who knows what benefits might therefrom flow?

Chapter Thirty Three

DOING THE RIGHT THING

Rights, responsibilities, and values.

Whether you're already in the CEO's chair or somewhere on the track to get there, you carry with you all the baggage you've picked up on the climb to where you want to be. Much of that baggage has been loaded on you by others – your professors, your colleagues, your mentors. Some of that baggage is good. It holds the tools you need to handle the challenges ahead. Some of it is bad. The bad stuff is the prejudices and conceits of the management generation you grew up in.

Unfair as it may seem, CEOs aren't a universally loved and respected lot. The excesses of the last two decades took care of that. There was a time, though, when CEOs were much better thought of than they are today. From shortly after World War II and well into the early eighties, there was a breed of CEO which seemed to have a broader view of their responsibilities than is now in vogue. This breed included men like Reg Jones, Irv Shapiro, Steve Bechtel, Edgar Kaiser, David Packard and many others these names will suggest to you. They acted as if a significant part of their charter was to build companies and create jobs so that people could do better, so that towns could prosper and good schools be available and decent housing somewhere within reach. They had a real concern for their employees. They were actively and personally involved in their communities, helping them grow, improving the quality of life. They made it a point to know their lawmakers and work with them. They didn't care for the press much more than you do, but they made themselves available and were effective when they had to be.

This breed recognized their obligation to their shareholders, but they acknowledged other obligations as well ...obligations to values not limited to the bottom line. There was a human-ness about them.

I think you're going to have to find this quality again to be successful in the new century.

This won't be easy. The pressures to increase shareholder values and the lure of rewards beyond the imagination of managers a generation ago will see to that. The mantra is already firmly in place—we work for the shareholder. The implication of this is that anything which advances shareholder value is good and anything which retards it is bad. The consequence is that decision making often gets reduced to the lowest common denominator, which is: If it doesn't maximize the bottom line, forget it.

You need to consider this. In a world of insecure, instantly informed people demanding more for themselves, carrying no loyalties to institutions, and skeptical of the intentions of the elite, you need to consider whether management can continue to hang its hat on the we-work-for-the-shareholder rack, justify its actions accordingly, and carry on as yesterday.

I wonder, instead, if the successful management of the new millenium isn't going to have to start demonstrating a heightened sense of responsibility to the societies at whose pleasure all companies exist, and, if necessary, even forego a penny-or-two a share now and then to achieve benefits its broader constituencies find desirable. I wonder if in so doing, management won't do better overall...maybe even make doing the right thing a competitive plus.

Arthur W. Page, an early AT&T executive who was one of the pioneers of reputation management, used to say, "All business in a democratic society begins with public permission and exists by public approval." The successful corporation, he believed, had to operate in the public interest, manage for the long run, and make customer satisfaction its primary goal. *"The successful corporation must,"* he said, *"conduct itself in such a way that the public will give it sufficient freedom to serve effectively."* Page held those views in the early 1930s.

I'm not suggesting you go soft. I'm suggesting you be smart. Listen to Page.

Chapter Thirty Four

MORTAL AFTER ALL

The problem for executives on their way to, or at, the top.

There was a custom in ancient Rome that when the victorious general returned from the wars, a triumphal entry was made into the city. Trumpets blared. Flower petals floated in the air. The assembled multitudes shouted and cheered as the hero rode proudly through the streets, the vanquished and the spoils of war strung out behind his chariot. In the midst of all this glory, a small man rode beside him, whispering in his ear, "You are mortal."

The men who rise to the top in business and industry, in government and academia, are somewhat Caesar like. They rule within their empires. They have power, privilege, and esteem. And, at least in the corporate world, the spoils of victory are princely indeed. They pay for this, though, in ways they often don't realize. They become insulated. They become insular. They lose touch.

The world that most CEOs and the senior executives of most major corporations live in is vastly different from the world of the publics they serve. The income and social and hierarchical disparities are considerable. While he may have come from humble beginnings, it doesn't take the successful executive long to get used to these things, and soon he begins to forget what it's like to be an ordinary person trying to get along, or put a kid through school, or find a way to care for an elderly parent. He loses his frame of reference with the real world beyond the executive suite.

This is one of the great problems for executives at or near the top of their organizations. Being surrounded by other executives much like himself, cushioned in an income layer that less than one percent of the overall population enjoys, and circulating in social and political circles of similar wealth and privilege, he comes to think that all reasonable men think as he and his colleagues think and that all responsible men understand the rightness of his actions. Which leads to some sorry miscalculations and stupid insensitivity.

The person in your organization most likely to keep you in touch with the world of real people is your CPRO. This is among the things he is trained for and paid to do. He's the one charged with having a finger on the pulse of all your constituencies. He'll know what's on their minds. He'll understand their expectations. If you have the right man in the job, he'll tell you what you need to know, not what he thinks you want to hear. If you're off base, he'll call it. If you're doing dumb things, he'll say so. You need a man like this. If you have one, treasure him. No one else in the organization is likely to tell the Emperor about his clothes. And the truth is what you need.

It will be more important in this new millenium than ever before for the men at the top of their organizations to understand and be personally in touch with their constituencies. Spurred by the claims of the wanting millions in the under-developed and developing countries and intensified by the demands of the affluent world, the emphasis, in this new age, is going to be on people, on meeting their needs and expectations. There isn't going to be much patience with lip-service or excuses. The currency of power will increasingly be information.

Among your constituents, everyone who wants it is going to have instant information on almost everything you and your company do. The stage you play on will be constantly lit and intensely scanned. While others look in, you must have the ability to look out – the ability to read the mood and drift of your constituent environment, to have the feel and know the smell of it.

Some of the research on actionable public opinion mentioned earlier can help you do this. Input from your CPRO will help give the human dimension to the decisions you have to make. But like most other matters of consequence that involve people in the new millenium, you'll have to be directly involved. You'll have to have personal contact with employees and customers and government officials. You'll have to talk with community and cultural leaders, and those in academia – not every now and then, but regularly. You'll have to ask questions. You'll have to *listen*!

In the process, you'll use Email, and the Intranet, and voice mail, and closed circuit inter-active TV bounced off satellites to let you have two way exchanges with customers, and employees, and stockholders, and even the media, everywhere you operate. You may even use focus groups assembled specifically to give you insight into particular problems and challenges.

You'll interface with people not in your income bracket or of your mind set, which, for the most part, describes most of your constituents. You'll do this regularly. You may get your hands a little dirty and work up a sweat now and again, but you'll be far better prepared to lead and to win.

The automatic response to this suggestion will probably be, "I don't have time for all this." Make the time. A man can't lead unless he can feel. He cannot feel unless he can touch.

That's the way it is with mortals.

Chapter Thirty Five

AND WE END IT WITH...

A few rules for the road.

The Clausen Canon: **Under promise. Over perform.**

The Maier Maxim: **Never make an important decision before you have to; you might miss the chance to make a better one. But don't dawdle. You may wind up having the decision made for you by time and events.**

The Byrd Assertion: **Convince my constituents. If they're for you, I'm for you. If they're against you, there's no way on God's green earth I'm going to support you.**

The Rhody Premise: **Timidity never won any ball games. Silence never swayed any masses. Take and hold the initiative.**

The Kissinger Postulate: **Truth is often the best alternative.**

The Sandberg Corollary to the Kissinger Postulate: **In matters of moment, truth is the only *smart* alternative.**

The Rule of the Real World: **Perceptions are what count.**

A LITTLE LIGHT READING

As I mentioned at the beginning, my intent with this book is to wake you up to the possibilities this discipline holds and lay out a few fundamental principles that can help you use it more effectively in sculpting the ends you seek.

If you want to know more, and there is incredibly more to know, there are tons of material out there to help you. Most of it is in the form of books – some excellent, some okay, and some awful. To help you through that forest, a short list of a few I like follows.

The Engineering of Consent ....**Edward L. Bernays**
(A fine collection of essays on the basics of the game by some of the pioneers in the field.)

Crowds & Power ....**Elias Canetti**
(A classic on the uses of power and mass psychology.)

Practical Public Affairs In An Era of Change
Edited by Lloyd Dennis
(Expert advice on the various tools available and how to use them from some of the most accomplished contemporary players.)

Crisis Response ....**Jack A. Gottschalk, editor**
(Excellent case studies of some of the worst contemporary crises—Bophal, the McDonald's St. Ysidro massacre, the AT&T network breakdown, the Gerber baby food scare, etc.) and how they were managed, or, in some cases, mismanaged.)

Rumor In The Marketplace ....**Frederick Koenig**
(A study of the damage rumors can do in the marketplace with guidelines for countermeasures.)

The Prince and the Discourses .... **Niccolo Machiavelli**
(The seminal work on power politics with lessons still valid today.)

Top Dog .... **J. David Pincus & J. Nicholas DeBonis**
(How successful CEOs use the tools of public relations to achieve their goals, with analysis of the styles of some well known contemporary leaders.)

Words & Values ....**Peggy Rosenthal**
("Dominant words" and how they direct actions and reactions.)

Rashomon And Other Stories ....**Akutaqawa Ryunosoke**
(the classic portrayal of the way of perceptions – or rent the film.)

POSTSCRIPT

Three world class professionals...Ed Block of AT&T, David Fausch of Gillette, and Bill Shepard of Alcoa; an old friend I grew up with in this field...Darden Chambliss of the Associated Press and The Aluminum Association; the best executive recruiter in the business and himself a professional...Bob Woodrum of Korn-Ferry; and one of the nation's leading public relations educators...Dr. Frank Kalupa of the University of Texas, reviewed this manuscript in its draft stages and, with their good sense and considerable experience, made invaluable contributions to the finished product. The conclusions expressed here are mine. They bear no responsibility for those. But their efforts in helping me be clear on what I want to say, and not unduly provocative, are appreciated more than I can tell them.

AND THANKS

This little book isn't quite grand enough to warrant a dedication, so I want to offer an acknowledgement instead.

Bob Sandberg of Kaiser Aluminum & Chemical Corporation, Bill Shepard of Alcoa, and Harry Towles, bless his heart, alas, now gone, of the Kentucky Department of Fish and Wildlife Resources, taught me how the game ought to be played and gave me opportunities to be as good as I could.

There are some debts too big to be repaid. Thank you, gentlemen. I'm beholden.

ABOUT THE AUTHOR

Ron Rhody's forty year career covers most of what there is to cover in the fields of public relations, reputation management, and strategic communications.

As chief executive of *rci,* he's worked with and advised CEOs and senior executives of *Fortune 500* companies on matters ranging from hostile take-overs to corporate repositioning, from operating disasters to major product launches. He's helped university boards of directors, heads of government agencies, and owners and managers of small companies and start-ups reach their objectives in good times and bad.

Prior to forming *rci* he was Executive Vice President and Director of Corporate Communications and External Affairs for BankAmerica Corporation and a member of its Senior Management Council. At Bank of America he was responsible for the corporation's public relations and communications strategies, policies, and programs during one of the most traumatic, and ultimately successful, decades in its history.

Before Bank of America, he was Corporate Vice President, Public Relations and Advertising for Kaiser Aluminum & Chemical Corporation and a member of the company's Managing Committee. There he directed the communications strategies for the intense marketing battles and international expansions and down-sizings endemic to the world-wide aluminum industry.

He worked as a daily newspaper reporter and columnist; as a radio and television newsman; and in state government in his native Kentucky before joining Kaiser.

Rhody's programs have earned many national and international honors, including Silver Anvils of the Public Relations Society of America, the Gold Quill of the International Association of Business Communicators, Oscars of Industry of *Financial World* magazine, the George Washington Medal of the Freedom Foundation, and Nicholson Awards of the National Association of

Investment Clubs. He was named Public Relations Professional of the Year by the professional journal *Public Relations News* in 1981; received the Harlow Award for outstanding professionalism in 1983; was selected one of the top ten U.S. professionals by *Public Relations Reporter*; received the International Association of Business Communicators Distinguished Communicator Award in 1989; was elected to the College of Fellows of the Public Relations Society of America in 1993; received the Lifetime Achievement Award of *Inside PR Magazine* in 1994; and the Hall of Fame Award of the Page Society, the national professional organization, in 1996. He is Founding Chairman of the San Francisco Academy, and past chairman of the Public Relations Seminar.

Wide-A-Wake (Hood Tales) Volume 1

Written By: Dwan Marquis Williams

Typesetter: Shonda Gray

ISBN: 978-1986847636

Published Novels by Dwan Williams

The Enemy Within

Connected to the Plug

Connected to the Plug Part 2

Connected to the Plug Part 3

Hood Tales Vol. 1(Wide-A-Wake)

Novels coming soon…

L-O-V-E

My Brother's Keeper (Promises are Made to be Broken)

Can't Have Your Cake and Eat It

Urban Tales Vol. 2 (Wide-A-Wake)

ACKNOWLEDGEMENT

I would like to give a special acknowledge to Shonda Gray for all of her hard work, love, and support she has shown and put into this project and others.

I would like to acknowledge my mother Carolyn J. Willliams, my cousins Torey Barnes and Erica Williams for holding me down and my Lil Brother Alex J. Williams for the brotherly love and support he's given me over the years. Also, I would like to thank everyone that has purchased and read my work. You all make it possible for me to keep doing what I do best.

Peace & blessing to you all.

Dedications

I dedicate this book to my family, friends, and everyone out there that has lost a loved one to senseless crime and murder. You all are in my prayers.

Lockdown Shout Outs:

I would like to shout out a few friends and associates that I have met along the way. Shout out to Jasper "J-Smooth" Allen, my uncle Freddie Dean doing time upstate (N.J.), Johan & Mike Farmer, Juney Barnes, Calvin Hinnant, Kimberly Floyd, Dennis Howard, Chris Murray, Tyrone Rogers, Howard "Onk" Phillips, Jerry Mercer, Longhead Terry, Willard "Fatty Bread" Alston my partner Polo out of Goldsboro, Alabama Biggs, my V.A. homies, Chee, Lil Rob, Tez, Dee, J.P., Neko, Truly Matthews, Murph, and Hasan Williams. If I forgot to mention you, don't get in your feelings. I've come across too many good soldiers to name you all. Just remember to keep it moving and hold your heads high to the sky until you make it back home!!

Wide-A-Wake

Hood Tales

Volume 1

Wide-A-Wake

Hood Tales

Volume 1

Kevin

Introduction

The sun was just rising as Kevin sat in a chair in his living room peeking out of his blinds. He hadn't stepped one foot out of his apartment in the past four days, not since the night he had yet another shootout. That made the third one in the past seven and a half months. He hoped and prayed that it would be the last one. He inhaled deeply, not knowing just how much longer he would be able to escape deaths grip.

On the fifth day, Kevin got tired of being cooped up in his apartment, so he decided to take a trip across town to visit his Uncle Freddie at his funeral parlor. It had been a long time since he had seen his favorite uncle. Coming up he use to love going to visit him at work. He mainly went there when he needed advice or when he wanted to get the 411 on the latest news on the streets but the main thing that really caught his attention and made it all worthwhile were the stories of the people he told that were about to be buried. On this occasion, Kevin needed to know if his uncle had heard anything about the shootout he was involved in a few days ago. Kevin knew that he had hit his mark, but what he didn't know was if he had a warrant out for his arrest or if his mark was dead or not. At that moment a lot of thoughts began to run through his head like, did his mark survive the hit, if so was he out there at that very moment seeking revenge for the plot and most important, why hadn't his girlfriend Diann called him? That thought alone made him furious. He grabbed his black hoodie and headed out the door to get some much-needed fresh air on his way to the parlor.

"Damn," Kevin cursed when he stepped out of his front door. He just remembered that he had to troop it since his car was in the body shop. A week prior, Diann had caught him creeping with one of her neighbors while Kevin thought she was at work. Needless to say she wasn't and scratched his car up from bumper to bumper, flattened all four tires and broke out all of his windows.

one of her neighbors while Kevin thought she was at work.

He shook his head as he threw on his hood and proceeded on his mission. He wasn't no fool though because before he left, he checked his Mac-11, put one in the chamber and made sure it was properly concealed before being on his way. There was no way that he was going to get caught slipping, by no means necessary.

"Yo," he called out as he ran out the alley into the middle of the street in an attempt to stop one of his homies that had sped by him in a hurry. Seeing that his attempt had failed, he dipped back into the alley unnoticed before any prying eyes could get a good glimpse of him. There was one thing Kevin didn't need in his life right now and that was for some nosey person to give his whereabouts.

Kevin jogged from one alley way to the other, deep in the shadows of the large brick buildings that outlined the streets. After making sure that the coast was clear, he took off running as fast as he could to the next cut. "Damn that was close," he said to himself once he took a seat in a long alley with his back to a fence that surrounded one of the neighborhood houses. It only took a few seconds for him to realize that the resting spot that he took wasn't a very good one. When he turned around, Kevin was face to face with one of the biggest and meanest pit bulls that he had ever laid eyes on in his life. He was grateful for the fence that separated them, because the dog snapped at him so quickly, the fence was the

9

only thing that stopped it from grabbing Kevin's face. Kevin stumbled back and fell on his ass. He looked to his right, the way he just come from, then looked to his left and saw a gigantic rat in search of something to snack on for the day and chose option number two. Any normal rat would've got out of the way of a much larger opponent, but not that rat. "Damn," Kevin cursed, hating the decision he just made when the rat made a loud hissing sound and showed all his teeth. Kevin leaped over the rat in the nick of time. He looked back one last time and picked up his speed, praying he make it to his uncle's parlor in one piece.

Kevin made it to his uncle's funeral parlor in record breaking time. He took off his hood as soon as he stepped into the building then looked around. It had been a long time since he last entered his uncle's place of business and by the looks of things he could tell business had been really good. The once bare floor was now fully carpeted, the dingy walls were now coated with fresh paint and the front room had two nice caskets sitting pretty and ready for viewing.

Kevin looked up and directed his attention to the last room on the right where he heard humming sounds coming from. He knew it had to be his Uncle Freddie because he loved to hum the song "I'm Coming Home" while he worked. When Kevin approached the door, he noticed that it was slightly ajar. He turned his body to the side and slid in, making sure he didn't make a sound. He knew how much his uncle hated to be disturbed while he was doing his job. The humming stopped as Freddie bent over the smaller casket and said a silent prayer. By the size of it, Kevin could tell it had to be a child inside and he immediately began to feel sad for the kid as he thought of the child Diann was carrying crossed his mind. He took a seat and quietly waited to hear the story his uncle was about to tell.

"Ole Sincere," Freddie began as he put his hand on the casket beside the smaller one. "How did you end yourself up in this situation here?"

"The next time my friend. Next time," Sincere repeated as he slowly crept through the intersection.

When he pulled up to the stop sign of the block he was suppose to make the first drop off, he thought about the consequences of what he was about to do. After taking another sniff of the white powder, all the fears he once consumed went out the window. "Fuck it," he decided as he rode through the crossing, cruised up the block and clean pass the building. Avoiding the second drop a well, he drove to his crib.

*   *   *

Sincere was glad that he decided to make a quick stop before he went home. "I finally caught up with this nigga," he said to himself as he pulled up curb side in front of Curt's trap house.

Curt was someone that used to buy weight from Sincere when he used to pinch off of the work that he delivered for Haitian Joe and after a while, since he came often, Sincere began fronting Cur the work. He recognized that was a big mistake because now he saw him less and less every week.

After putting his car in park, Sincere dipped the bill into the bag of powder and took another toot. The young hustler was so busy serving the line of fiends, he never noticed Sincere pull up until the passenger side window of his Beamer came down and he called out his name. "Yo Curt, let me holla at you for a minute!"

"Damn," Curt mumbled under his breath. He hated the fact that he had got caught slipping with so much money in his pocket. He planned on stalling Sincere out as least for another three or four days. He watched Sincere turn the volume up on the steering wheel, then hit the button on the center console, and the window went up. After serving the next customer in line, Curt directed his attention to Sincere's car. He knew he had to go face the music, so he told the next customer in line to wait a minute and headed down the walk way. He thought about sliding a knot or two to one of them but decided against it, because if they ran off with it, that would have been like paying double once he replaced it, besides, he couldn't tell if Sincere was watching him or not because of the 5% tint that covered the windows.

Sincere was on his third dip into the bag of powder when Curt came knocking on the window. Sincere looked to the passenger's side window, took one more toot, then wiped his nose before unlocking the door. By the time Curt sat down, Sincere had checked his nose in the rearview mirror to make sure he had no sign of indulging before he address the issue at hand. "It's been a whole week little homie and you haven't got at me yet. What's going on with you?" Sincere asked once he turned down the volume on the radio.

"I-I-I was just about to call you later on tonight," Curt stuttered as he got his lie together.

"Tonight huh," Sincere questioned with his mouth turned to the side.

"For real! Things just started picking up, see," Curt said pointing to the long line of fiends that waited for him to step out the car to serve them. The real reason that Curt was taking so long to pay Sincere his money was because he had fucked a lot of it up the other night gambling. He had way more than enough money in his stash to pay Sincere and cop some more work but he didn't want to buy any dope as long as he was getting it fronted to him.

"Yea I see the trap house jumpin like a mutha fucka," Sincere admitted with a smile on his face. Curt thought that he was buying his story, but little did he know, Sincere had other plans in mind. "Let me get what you got on you now and I'll come by and get the rest later on tonight." Sincere turned to face Curt with his hand out waiting to get paid. After Curt pulled out the money in his pocket and handed it over, Sincere unfolded the bills to count them. "This ain't nothing but four grand," Sincere stated turning the money looking at both sides like more was going to pop up from somewhere.

"I know big homie. I got 9 ounces left in the house bagged up right now that I'm working on," Curt explained. Sincere was tired of playing the cat and mouse game with Curt and decided that he wasn't leaving unless he had all of the money and dope that Curt owed him.

"Don't even worry about it little homie," Sincere waved him off. That was like music to Curt's ears, until Sincere finished what he had to say. "Come on. Let's go in the house and get those 9 because I got somebody that want it right now." Curt's heart dropped when Sincere reached under his seat and retrieved a black Glock. Once he put one in the chamber, he opened his door and stepped out. By the time Sincere made it to the passenger side door, Curt hadn't moved a muscle. Not because he didn't want to but because he was afraid of what might happen when they got inside. "Come on," Sincere rushed then pulled the passenger's side door open. Curt reluctantly got out then closed the door behind him.

Curt led the way pass the long line of fiends that awaited his return. To their disappointment, Curt walked right passed them and into the trap house with Sincere right on his heels with his hand inside of his jacket.

To Sincere's surprise, the trap house was nothing what he expected. It was cleaner than any other spot that he had been in. Not to mention that he had all of the latest gadgets lying around in brand new boxes. He made a mental note to snatch up a few things on the way out, just for Curt having him to wait all of that time. Sincere kept his hand on the handle of his pistol as he followed Curt to the room in the back, just in case he tried anything stupid.

"What's going on?" Faith asked as she entered the room. She could tell that something was wrong when he turned around. She could see the stress lines in his forehead and by the look in his eyes, she knew that he was high as a kite. That was one thing that she hated about her husband. It had become an everyday thing for the past few weeks. The twitch in the corner of his mouth would always give him away.

"I can't explain right now, just trust me." That was what she was most afraid of. The last time she trusted him, they ended up in a shootout. She reluctantly exited out of the room, passed Knowledge crying in his high chair and in to his room to get his things together. Within ten minutes flat, they had everything they intended on taking with them and was out the door.

"You gonna tell me where we're going and why we had to leave in such a hurry now?" Sincere didn't reply right away. He just kept looking in the rearview mirror then back to the road in front of him. "You know my parents are going to have a fit when they come to pick Knowledge up and we're not there right? You at least could've let me call them to let them know that we wouldn't be there this weekend." He knew he couldn't keep the reason for them up and leaving from Faith for much longer. Faith sat silently waiting for Sincere to give her an explanation. She just hoped he hadn't done what he had been talking about doing for the past few weeks. Not wanting to upset him, she decided to come at him another way for the information. "So how was the drop today?" Sincere hated the fact that she knew all about his business. After getting no response, her biggest fear was confirmed. "Please tell me you didn't do what I think you've done?" Tired of hearing Faith's mouth, he finally flipped out.

"Man fuck dat fat ox tail eating mutha fucka. He got me out here delivering all this shit that could possibly end up with me serving a fuckin life sentence in the pen while he sittin back on his fat ass reaping all the damn benefits." He was so enraged, saliva was falling from his mouth. "And for what?" he asked, not really expecting an answer. "For crumbs, that's what!" She just sat there quiet and afraid to speak. She remembered what happened to her eye the last time she put her two cents where it wasn't wanted or needed.

"So what now?" she asked as her heart began to beat out of control. Faith thought of the stories that she'd heard about and what happened to the people that crossed Haitian Joe but to actually be a participant on the receiving end of the stick was a totally different experience. She was brought back to reality by the sound of Sincere's voice.

"So now we go to the airport, get on our plane and head as far west as we possibly can go. I was thinking about California. I got a cousin named Steve out there that'll let us stay at one of his cribs until we get settled in our own spot. What you think about that?"

slept with the engine running all night. Looking at the gas needle he knew he had to go to a gas station and soon. He looked to his right and began to nudge Faiths leg. "What man?" she asked with an attitude.

"Wake up we gotta go!" She sat up as he put the car in drive. Instead of going to a gas station, a thought crossed Sincere's mind so he headed to Mel Ski's house.

Mel Ski and Sincere were friends from way back in the days. Sincere turned him on to Haitian Joe shortly after he got put on. The only difference between the two was that Mel couldn't seem to stay on. Mainly because of his bad gambling habit.

"Yo I need a favor," Sincere explained when Mel Ski opened the door to let him in.

"Well good fuckin morning to you too,' Mel Ski joked as he closed the door behind him. "How can I assist you?" They both took a seat on Mel Ski's worn out sofa that had seen better days.

"I need a favor like I was saying." After seeing his friend wasn't in a joking mood Mel Ski became serious.

"Anything Bruh," Mel Ski replied, scooting to the edge of his seat to hear what Sincere needed of him.

"Yeah I bet," Sincere thought as he cut his eyes in Mel Ski's direction. He knew the only reason that Mel Ski was so eager to help him out was because he owed him ten grand for a debt he had paid Money's Loan Sharks a few weeks ago to not kill his ass.

"I need to borrow your car." Mel shot him a look as if he was asking too much since his car was worth much more than he owed. After letting him know he could pick it up at RDU International Airport the next day, he reluctantly agreed. That and because Sincere gave him an extra two G's. As soon as the money exchanged hands Mel was thinking of the card game he would be attending in a few hours.

Once Sincere switched rides he felt a lot safer, but just like every other nigga from the hood, Mel kept his car on "E." Stopping at the gas station was definitely not a part of his plan. There was one thing he knew for sure and that was he was not about to stop in town to get any. The thought of getting caught up at a gas pump while pumping gas sent shivers up his spine. He jumped straight on HWY 264 heading west with his fingers crossed. As he crossed I-95, he almost side swiped a car as he sped in front of the gas pump at the Citgo service station.

Sincere was scared as hell as he stood at the back of the car pumping gas. He looked up at every car that passed to make sure Haitian Joe wasn't on his trail. When he finished, he hurried in to the store to pay for the gas, get a few snacks for his family and to use the restroom. The first thing he did when he entered the restroom was splash water over his face. He was hoping that would wake him from the nightmare he was in but he was wrong. After seeing things were real, he went in to his pocket to retrieve the only thing he knew that could take away the worries, his nose candy. Before coming out, he checked his nose to make sure that there were no signs of residue from the two lines he had just sniffed. The last thing he needed at that time was for Faith to start tripping and blow his high.

When he made it back to the car he was relieved. He couldn't believe that they had made it that far without any signs of Haitian Joe or his goons. "Here, spark the blunt up." Sincere knew a blunt of Dro would take some of the edge off of Faiths attitude. "I guess not," he thought to himself when she didn't take it. He pulled out his lighter and put fire to it, then took a long pull. He called himself trying to be funny and blew a huge cloud of smoke in her direction. He knew how much she hated that, but he didn't care. At that point he just wanted for her to say something. It didn't matter if it was just to curse him out. After she didn't say anything he glanced over in her direction. When the smoke cleared the air, he lost what little food he had in his stomach from the day before. There sat Faith with a blank expression on her face with her throat slit from ear to ear. What really made him sick was that her tongue was hanging from it. He quickly looked in to the back seat only to find an empty car seat. When Sincere turned back around to get his gun from his waistline he was met by the barrel of Dreads sawed-off shotgun.

Dread was Haitian Joes main hitman. Whenever there was a situation that needed to be handles, he would handle it. He always wore a long black trench coat, black gloves and a black skully no matter the time of year and that day was no different. Sincere actually thought he would've seen him much sooner.

"Make my day," Dread threatened as he pumped the bottom of he shotgun barrel. Without showing any mercy Dread took the butt of the gun and slammed it into the side of his face. Dazed, Sincere reached for the steering wheel, missing it twice before finding it. Blood ran down the left side of his face like water from a hose as Haitian Joe entered the car and sat right behind him. It was then he realized that Mel had sold him out. He made a vow to kill him and anyone he loved, if he made it out alive.

"Look at what you made me do," Joe said in a calm like voice. He reached up in the front seat and removed a loose strand of hair out of Faith's face admiring her beauty. Haitian Joe truly had no remorse for what he had just done. "And to just think. I was about to promote your dumb ass." Haitian Joe hit Sincere over the back of the head making a lump appear on impact. Tears began to come down Sincere's face. Not because of the pain he was feeling or because he was afraid of what was about to happen to him, but because the stupid decision he made to take Haitian Joe's shit caused him, his wife, and son's life. "Were my shit at?" Joe asked in a tone to let Sincere know he was tired of talking. When he got

When Kevin entered in to the next room, he noticed three more caskets that were set up and ready to be viewed. "What happened to them?" he asked as he reached over on the podium beside him and grabbed the one big obituary that contained all of the information on the deceased. Kevin took a seat in the front row and began thumbing through it. "I remember him," he said to himself, remembering the young kid that passed by his house everyday tossing a football in the air on the way to and from the school bus stop.

"This one here name was T.J.," Freddie began then rested his hand on top of the casket that sat in the middle of the other two. "Another one of our young, black youth robbed of a promising future. It all began on his last day of school."

T.J

Blood In Blood Out

T.J. smiled to himself as he made his way out of the school doors with his report card in hand. He couldn't believe that he was going to be a freshman in college at the end of the summer. The only thing he had to do now was figure out what he was going to do for a job this summer while he waited.

On his way home, he had to walk through one of the roughest neighborhoods in the city, Maplewood, also known as the Ave. Some people called it Little Jamaica because everyone in the hood wore their hair in dreadlocks, also for its high crime rate. "Aye Yo T.J!" a familiar voice called out from behind him. T.J. stopped in his tracks and slowly turned around to see who could possibly be calling his name in that neighborhood. A smile crept upon his face when he saw his old friend Kool Breeze jogging across the street in his direction.

"Kool Breeze," T.J. responded. They showed each other love with a hand shake and a short embrace before they stepped back and looked each other up and down. "I see that you're out here doing your thang." T.J. was referring to the diamond infested cross that hung from the 40" cable around Kool Breezes neck.

"Ah man this ain't shit. Wait til you see the one I'ma cop by the end of next week," Kool Breeze boasted as he held up the charm and looked at it. T.J. was almost blinded by the reflection from the sun rays as it beamed off of the flawless stones. "Where you on your way to?" Kool Breeze asked snapping him out of his daydream.

"To the crib. I got to fill out a few more applications to some colleges for the upcoming year. I got four scouts looking at a brother already," he confessed before popping his collar. "You know your boy is going to be the next Julius Peppers," T.J. bragged as they both turned then headed up the block. Kool Breeze was proud of his friend. He sometimes wished that he would've stayed in school, but unlike T.J., he was good at hustling, not sports.

"I know that's right," Kool Breeze agreed. "Don't forget about the small people when you make it to the big league," he joked as they approached the corner.

"Come on dawg. Don't even try to play me like that. I'll never forget where I come from," T.J. promised.

"Dat's wasup." Kool Breeze knew his best friend was telling the truth. Before they could start talking about the old times that they use to share together coming up, their conversation got interrupted by another one of their old friends, Timmy.

Timmy, Kool Breeze, and T.J. all grew up together in the same ...ood as kids. Timmy being a slight bit older than them tended to ...ometimes venture off and test the waters with the older kids.

"Yo, I'll be right back in a jiffy," Timmy promised Kool Breeze ...nd T.J. when he saw a couple of older kids walk off between the ...ec building and rest room. They watched Timmy join the so-...alled "Cool Kids" that were known for selling drugs and getting ...igh. Fifteen minutes later, Timmy returned, looking spaced out. ...hey didn't pay much attention until Timmy stood in the same ...pot, staring off into space, looking at nothing when they walked ...ff.

"Timmy," Kool Breeze called his name, trying to get his ...ttention, but it didn't work.

"Come on man. Stop playing," T.J. told him as they made their ...vay back over to their friend. Even though they stood directly in ...immy's face, it was like he was looking right through them. "I'm ...oing to go get Mrs. Estelle," T.J. told Kool Breeze then took off ...unning down the street to Timmy's house to get his grandma. ...When T.J. and Mrs. Estelle returned, Timmy had come down off ...f his high a little and Kool Breeze had talked him into sitting ...lown on the ground with him.

"Chile what is wrong wit chu?" Mrs. Estelle questioned her ...grandson, bending down and looking in his glassy eyes. Having ...aised eight children of her own, she knew immediately what he

35

had gotten into. SMACK! "Get chu" ass up and get in dat damn house," she smacked and scolded him. Out of nowhere, Timmy regained all of his strength and senses.

"What did you do that for," he questioned, holding the right side of his face. "I ain't even did nuthin." Kool Breeze and T.J. watched their best friend walk off in tears. When he was out of sight, Kool Breeze looked at T.J. and burst out into laughter.

"Did you see how that nigga got some act right in him when Mrs. Estelle tapped dat Jaw?" Kool Breeze asked his homie as they walked off in the other direction heading for the Jew store to go steal some lemon heads and jaw breakers. T.J. on the other hand didn't see what was so funny.

"Did you see how spaced out he was looking before Mrs. Estelle hit him? What if he do it again? He might turn into one of them base heads we see that be looking like skeletons and stuff," T.J. said, worried about is friend.

"Ahhh, that nigga gonna be alright. After Mrs. Estelle whip dat ass when they get in the house, he won't try it again, believe me!" Kool Breeze answered, remembering when his mother gave Mrs Estelle permission to beat him the last time him and Timmy got caught stealing out of the Jew store a few months back.

"Your're probably right," T.J. agreed. Deep down inside he hoped that his friend wouldn't get hooked on drugs. A few months

ter, word had gotten back to Kool Breeze and T.J that their best
iend had kirked out on a joint laced with cocaine, and shortly
fter that he had graduated from lacing to smoking crack straight
om the pipe.

*   *   *

"Kool Breeze. You got a twenty?" T.J. looked at Timmy and
ouldn't believe his eyes. He had lost so much weight since the
ist time he had seen him. The only thing that hadn't changed was
he large scar that covered his neck from when they all were
ounger, and Timmy ran into a bobbed wire clothes line.

"Timmy," T.J. called out to his longtime friend. Timmy looked
ver to T.J. with a gapped tooth smile. He hadn't even noticed T.J.
tanding right next to him until then.

"What's up T.J," he acknowledged shamefully. Timmy could
ee the disappointment written all over his face but the thought of
is next high outweighed his friends feelings as he turned back
owards Kool Breeze to score his hit. "I need to holla at you in
rivate for a minute." They took a few steps from T.J. and made
heir transaction. Once it was done, Timmy took one last look at
.J., held his head down low and headed up the block to get his
last on. Kool Breeze walked back over to T.J while neatly
lacing the twenty dollars he'd just made with the rest of his

money. Just as T.J. was about to question Kool Breeze about Timmy, another fiend swiftly walked up to them.

"Let me get a sixteenth," he asked with an uncontrollable twitch in the left side of his mouth.

"How much you got?" Kool Breeze asked as he reached in his crotch where he stashed his crack to retrieve the order. The fiends eyes almost popped out of its sockets when he saw all the crack inside of the ziplock bag. He scratched at his arms and chest anticipating the fix he was about to receive. "How much fool. I ain't got all day," he barked at the crackhead. Still scratching, the fiend began explaining.

"I know you said you wanted two hundred for the tenth but I'm a little short this time." He shuffled from one foot to the other, praying Kool Breeze would show a little pity for him this time around. Kool Breeze had a feeling that the fiend was going to try and pull a stunt on him but he wasn't trying to hear it. He already owed him a hundred dollars from last week so he wasn't about to add another dime to his existing bill.

"Get the fuck outta here. You already in the red mutha fucka. I should hit you upside your head and take what you owe me but I don't want to make it hot out here," Kool Breeze threatened as he began to place the bag back in his stash spot. Before he knew what happened, the fiend snatched the bag of crack and took off running in the opposite direction. "Yo grab that fiend," he called out to

T.J. Little did the fiend know, he picked the wrong day to snatch and run. Before he was halfway up the block, T.J. had tackled him to the ground where he and Kool Breeze commenced to beating the poor fiend to death. "You thought you could snatch my shit and get away with it," Kool Breeze asked through clenched teeth. The fiend balled up in the fetal position to block as many of the punches as he could. Just when he thought it was over, they stood over him and began kicking the shit out of him. The only thing that saved the fiend was the sound of an engine racing their way full speed.

"5-0," T.J. shouted and then took off running between two abandoned houses. Kool Breeze was dead on his heels before the police could bring his cruiser to a halt and jump out. There was no way that the officer would dare pursue the two suspects on foot after he heard tales of the last officers that tried to do such a thing like that in the same neighborhood. That was cool with Kool Breeze. Besides, he already had a pending drug case in the courts and the loaded .45 he had on him would've sent him away forever.

"Man that shit was close as hell," T.J. admitted once they entered his bedroom. He was glad that his mother was still at work because she would've asked a thousand and one questions of why they busted in her house out of breath. Kool Breeze closed the bedroom door behind them then took a seat at the foot of T.J's bed.

re-up with me and only me. Do we got an understanding?" T.J. agreed as he continued listening to the instruction Money was giving him. "When you're finished, get in touch with Kool Breeze, then we can start business together. Any questions?" T.J. couldn' believe his ears. He was finally connected.

"Sounds like a plan. I promise you that you won't regret this." T.J. was about to turn around to leave before Money stopped him.

"For this you will owe me one. When the time comes, I'll get in touch with you." Instead of walking back home, Money gave T.J. a ride. It was more for precaution. He didn't want T.J. getting stopped and harassed by the police with a pocket full of rocks. Besides, he needed to know where his latest investment lived.

"So this is where you stay?" Money asked when he pulled up to the address that T.J. had given him.

"Yep," T.J. replied then leaned between to two front seats and gave Money and Kool Breeze some dap. Money watched T.J. make his way onto the porch and into the house before putting the truck in drive.

"Perfect," Money said to himself as he thought about how his plan was all falling into place.

T.J. walked into the house and hurried to his room to stash away the drugs since his mother hadn't made it home from work

et. He looked at the time on his watch and knew he didn't have
ong.

No sooner than he finished placing the shoe box full of crack at
he back of this closet, he heard his mother call out his name as she
entered the house. "T.J.! You home?"

"Yeah. I'll be right out," he answered, stepping out of the his
closet and closing the door behind him. By the time he unlocked
and opened his room door his mother was standing right there.

"What you say?" T.J. smiled at his mother playing the though
parent role.

"I meant yes Ma'am," he corrected himself.

"That's more like it. You know I raised you better than that,'
she said then finished with a smile. "Get ready for dinner." T.J.
watched his mother head to the kitchen to prepare dinner then
headed to the bathroom to wash off.

After dinner, they went into the living room and watched
elevision together like they always did when they were home at
he same time. Hours had passed, and T.J. found himself staring at
his sleeping mother and thought about how lucky he was to have
her in his life. Seeing the small chill bumps covering her arms,
T.J. walked over to the closet and pulled a blanket out then laid it
on top of her. "Now it's my turn to take care of you from here on
out," he whispered then kissed her on top of her forehead. When

T.J. walked out of the living room to go to his bedroom, his mother wiped the tears from her eyes.

"I know you will," she said with pride. Little did she know, he had just entered the most dangerous game of his life, and it didn't involve any kind of sports.

When T.J. entered his room, he headed straight for his closet to get the shoe box full of drugs out and began to break it down. He had so much he wanted to do with the money, being that he had to go off to school. He knew they money he saved would take a lot of the burden off of his mother. His mind also thought about the latest gear that he was going to buy to take to school with him. He couldn't wait to go to the basketball games that were held at the park in the summers. After putting the shoe box back into the closet, T.J. climbed into bed with a smile on his face.

The crack was selling like candy. It was so good that T.J. ran out in two days. His bankroll was increasing steadily and by the end of the week he had flipped the ounce that Money had given him three times and now had his block on lock. Everything seemed to be going fine until he received an unexpected phone call. "Yo kid. You ready to turn in that favor you owe me?" Money asked

"No doubt," T.J. responded, as he stopped counting his doe, ready to put in work.

"That's what I'm talking about. A man of his word. Meet me at the park in like a hour," Money instructed. Before T.J. could agree, Money cut him off. "And don't be late," he warned before disconnecting the call. As soon as Money hung up, T.J. went into his closet, pulled out his Timberland shoe box then placed the money inside. Once he secured it back in its spot, T.J. hurried out the door and to the park not wanting to disappoint his big homie.

When Money pulled up to the park, T.J. was expecting to see Kool Breeze in the truck with Money, but he wasn't. He climbed into the passenger side of the truck once it stopped in front of him. "Baby let me call you back in a few while I handle my business," Money told the caller on the other end as T.J. hopped in. "I love you too," he lied before disconnecting the call and directing his attention to T.J. "You ready young blood?" T.J. looked over at Money with confidence before responding.

"No doubt big homie." He rubbed his hands together as he waited for Money to give him instructions on what he wanted him to do. He couldn't wait to prove to Money that he was a man of his word. "What you need for me to do?" Proud of his response, Money began to break down the situation.

"There's a guy by the name of Ty-Boogie that has become like a real thorn in my side since we went our separate ways. He needs to be taught a lesson on sticking his nose where it don't belong, you feel me?" T.J. nodded his head in agreement.

47

out of her for disrespecting his ride but remembered he had something to do.

"I'll get her ass next time," he promised as he took the key to the truck out of his pocket. Just when he was about to stick it in the ignition, his passenger side door reopened. Thinking it was Blondie he said, "Bitch didn't I tell you," then paused in mid-sentence when he saw the barrel of T.J.'s gun pointed in his face. He couldn't believe that he got caught slipping as he threw both hands in the air. "I'ma kill that bitch," was the first thought that came to his mind. Thinking fast on how to get out of his tight situation, Ty-Boogie did what he did best, talk. "Yo youngin, you can have the money," he offered. By the look in T.J.'s eyes he knew it wasn't about the money but he was determined to make it out alive. "All I need is a little distraction and I know I can make it to my hammer under my seat," he reasoned wanting to make an example out of the kid in front of him. T.J. tried to squeeze the trigger but when he looked into Ty-Boogies eyes, he began to have second thoughts. It was something about the man in front of him that wouldn't let him do it. T.J. pulled the hammer back trying to find the courage, but none was there.

"I can't do this," he finally concluded. Just as he lowered his gun, opened the truck door and slid out, the front door to the gambling spot swung open. When he turned around, he and Blondie locked eyes before she let out a blood curling scream.

That one second ended up being a fatal one, not for T.J., but for
Ty-Boogie. He came up from under his seat a second too late. T.J.
let a round off into the middle of Ty-Boogie's forehead, ending his
life instantly. T.J. turned his attention to the screaming Blondie
and debated on whether or not to end her life as well since she saw
his face. "No witnesses, no murder," he decided and started up the
steps in her direction. Blondie was planted in one spot as if she
was standing in the middle of a concrete slab. As T.J. lifted his
gun arm, he heard several footsteps rushing to the door making
him duck between two houses and disappeared into the night. He
ended up on the next street over, unnoticed, making a clean get
away.

   T.J. took all of the short cuts that he could remember until he
made it to his street. He smiled when he seen his house in the
middle of the block with all of the lights off. "Good she's sleep,"
he said to himself, not knowing how to explain to his mother why
he was coming in so late. As soon as he stepped into his front
yard, he felt his cell vibrate so he looked down and read his text:
Good job Young Blood. "How did he know that I did it already?"
T.J. asked himself then looked around. That's when he saw
Money's truck pull away from the stop sign and cross the
intersection. T.J. turned and walked into the house, and just like he
figured, his mother was fast asleep on the sofa. After blowing her
a kiss he headed to the bathroom to take a shower.

THE NEXT MORNING

T.J. was awakened by the smell of bacon, cheese eggs, and grits lingering in the air. He smiled when the aroma of freshly made buttermilk biscuits assaulted his nostrils. He drug his exhausted body out of bed and headed to the bathroom to freshen up so he could join his mother at the breakfast table. "Good morning sleepy head," Ann greeted T.J. once he entered the kitchen. T.J. couldn't understand how she always knew when he entered into a room that she was in, especially when he made sure not to make a sound.

Ann was a single mother of one. She did whatever she had to do to make ends meet for her and her son. Even if that meant working two jobs. The two of them had a very special bond between each other. They talked about everything under the sun and never worried about being judged by the other.

"Good morning to you too ma," he replied as he made his way over to the stove beside her. T.J. watched as Ann pulled the pan of biscuits out of the oven then kissed her on her cheek. As soon as she placed them on top of the stove, T.J. attempted to reach for one of them.

"Boy I know you didn't just try to put those filthy hands on my darn biscuits did you?" She scolded him after popping the back of his hand. T.J. smiled and held his hands up in the air.

"My hands ain't dirty," he claimed then showed her each side. Ann looked at her son wide eyed before he realized his mistake. "I meant they are not dirty," he corrected his language. After Ann raised both brows, T.J. knew he wasn't getting any breakfast until he washed his hands in front of her. "Okay, okay," he gave in and walked over to the kitchen sink to wash his hands. By the time he was finished, Ann had both of their plates set at the table.

After they ate breakfast, T.J. washed the dishes while Ann went into the living room to rest her feet. When he was finished cleaning up, T.J. went in and joined his mother on the couch where she was flipping through the channels to find something to watch. "Let me handle this." T.J. grabbed the remote out of Ann's hand and began to channel surf.

"Turn back," Ann demanded and sat at the edge of the sofa. T.J. turned back to the local news channel and listened in on the latest news on what had occurred the night before.

"Good morning everyone. This is Zhaliah Thompson reporting live from the corner of Vance and Ash Street, a well known gambling house called Good Daddy's," she pointed to the shotgun house behind her before carrying on. "This is where Tyrese Dawson's body was found, slumped in his truck with a bullet in the middle of his forehead. Tyrese Dawson, also know on the streets as the infamous Ty-Boogie, was one of Wilson's most vicious kingpins. The police haven't ruled out robbery even thing, we're even, no strings attached, got it?" Kool Breeze inhaled deep before speaking again.

"Okay. I'll tell'em but I don't think he's gonna be pleased with your decision." Out of curiosity Kool Breeze asked, "Why do you want out so bad?" T.J. thought long and hard about how to tell his friend his reason before breaking it down.

"Because Ty-Boogie was my father." Kool Breeze was caught totally by surprise. All the years of knowing T.J., he thought that T.J.'s father was dead. T.J. ran down the exact story that his mother ran down to him to the very T. Kool Breeze felt T.J.'s pain and knew exactly where he was coming from.

"I got you homie," he assured his friend before ending the call. T.J. decided to take a long walk to clear his mind from all the drama that had happened over the summer. He couldn't wait to receive the letter to find out what college accepted him.

Later on that night when T.J. returned home, Ann was sitting in the living room waiting on him. "Why are you sitting in the dark?" he asked as he walked through.

"You okay," she asked as he made his way over to the couch beside her. They both sat in the dark lost in their own thoughts until he answered.

"Yea. I'm good." Feeling a bit awkward, T.J. rose to his feet and stood in front of his mother. He wanted to say so much but no words would come out. It pained him that his mother would hold something so important away from him. He thought about all of the football games he played and wished both of his parents were here to cheer him on like his other teammates.

"Baby I know you're probably mad with me right now but believe me when I tell you that I did it for your own good," she explained with teary eyes. T.J. wasn't in the mood to talk about it at the time, so he put on a fake smile then told her.

"I'm tired Ma. I just want to go lay down and rest. We'll talk about this another time," he promised. He didn't wait for a response before turning on his heels and heading to his room. "Did anyone call," he yelled out without breaking a stride.

"Yes. Your friend Jamarielle," she replied as he reached the end of the hall. Seconds later she heard the door slam and the sounds of music coming from his stereo system. "I love you Tyrese Jr.," Ann whispered before praying that things between her and her son would somehow get better.

T.J. picked up the cordless phone and dialed Kool Breeze's number before taking a seat at the foot of his bed. "Yo where you been man?" I've been trying to reach you all day," Kool Breeze answered before T.J. could get a word in.

"I been out homie. I had a lot on my mind." Kool Breeze instantly felt guilty when he thought about the situation his friend was in.

"Yea I feel you." There was a moment of silence as T.J. flashed backed to the moment he pulled the trigger on his father. He remembered the look in his father's lifeless eyes as they stared at him. He snapped out of his daze when he heard the sound of Kool Breeze's voice in the receiver.

"You hear me T.J.?" Once he was sure he had T.J.'s attention, he continued. "Money wants you to meet him at the abandoned house on Vick Street at eight o'clock in the morning." T.J. wondered why he wanted him to meet him in an abandoned house. "Once you do this last thing, you'll be out of the game for good with no strings attached," Kool Breeze assured him. Now all he had to do was try and get some sleep without visioning his father's face before he took his last breath.

It was 6:30 in the morning when Ann poked her head into T.J.'s bedroom. That was something that she always did every morning before she headed to work. He laid there quietly in his bed with the covers over his head. Any other day he would've stuck his head from under the covers to see her off but not today. Not able to take his silence anymore, Ann backed out of his room with a long tear streaming down her cheek. Once she was gone, T.J. removed the covers from over his head. A few seconds later, he heard the front door then close. He didn't get out of bed until he heard the familiar sound of Ann's car starting and pulling out of their driveway. Within the next hour, he was dressed and on his way to Vick Street.

A half hour later, T.J. turned the corner of Green and Vick. He spotted the abandoned house on the right hand side and proceeded in its direction. He was more nervous now than ever, wondering if his fate was near. Truth be told, he really didn't want to get out of the family. The entire walk to Vick Street all T.J. could hear was the sound of Money telling him that nothing was more important than family and the way that Money took him in like he was his son, made it even harder. T.J. made his way to the back of the house and climbed the back steps. "Did he know that Ty-Boogie was my father," he asked himself for the thousandth time. "Nah, he couldn't have known," he reasoned. As soon as he crossed the back door threshold, T.J. called out Money's name.

"In here," he replied from one of the front rooms in the house. T.J. made his way down the hall and stuck his head in every room until he found the one Money was in. As he approached, he could see the disappointment in Money's eyes. "You ready to handle your business?" Money asked when they were face to face. When T.J. confirmed that he was, Money walked by him and out the door to the room across the hall from where they were. When they made it to the next room, it was so dark, T.J. couldn't even see is hands when he held them in front of him, do to the wooden planks that covered the windows in the room. His heart began to beat out of control and he found it hard for him to breath. "You strapped?" Money asked once he lit a match that illuminated the room with light then placed it to a candle that sat in the middle of the floor.

"Yea," T.J admitted lifting his shirt to show the butt of the gun he used to kill his father.

"Good," he replied then led the way to the closet door across the room. T.J. followed with a confused look on his face. They stopped short a foot away from the door before Money turned around and faced him. "You sure you ready?" Money asked one last time. T.J. just wanted to get things over with so he could go home and go on with his life and leave all that behind him. T.J. nodded and Money stepped to the side to give him a clear view of what he had to do.

"Mmmmmmm,mmmmmm," the person mumbled as they tried to squirm out of the chair they were tied in, almost knocking it to the floor. T.J.'s hands shook uncontrollably as he lifted it up to the side of the victim's head. He was glad that Money had a pillow case over the head of his victim because he knew if he had to look into their pleading eyes, he wouldn't be able to do it.

"Do it son," Money coached as he stood by his side.

"Mmmmmmm,mmmmmmm," the victim moaned, scaring T.J. half to death. T.J. closed his eyes and a single teardrop rolled down his cheek. When it hit the floor. He pulled back on the trigger and sent a bullet straight into the pillow case. He opened his eyes and what once was a white pillow case became completely red as blood ran from the bottom of it. He stood there in a daze as blood formed all around his feet and watched as the body convulsed. When it finally stopped, he turned around to ask Money was they even, but he was gone.

It was nightfall when T.J. made it home. He sat at the park all daylong thinking about the events that happened in his life since the last day of school. He was glad that everything was finally over now. He walked up to his door and checked the mailbox that hung to the right. A smile appeared on his face when he saw a letter from a major college that he had applied for. He was halfway down the hall when he ripped the envelope open and read the words "accepted" right above the words "full scholarship."

UNC wanted him for football. "Yes," he shouted at the top of his lungs. Things were starting to look up for him and there wasn't anyone he wanted to share his news with besides his mother. Even thought he was still upset with her, Ann had worked her ass off to make sure he made it to every practice, even when he didn't want to go. She was the one that pushed him to study harder, just in case things didn't go as planned in sports. "MAAA," he shouted and stormed to her room, only to find it empty. He headed to the kitchen and then the living room. When he came up empty in those places as well, he came to the conclusion that she had worked a double shift.

T.J. ended up falling asleep watching old re-runs of Good Times as he waited for Ann to come home. He was awakened by this news caster for the morning news with breaking news. "Hello everybody. This is Kadijah Williams here reporting live from the scene of yet another gruesome murder in the past few days." T.J. wiped the coal out of his eyes then sat up to get a better view. He knew they were talking about the murder he had committed and wanted to know if they had any leads. "I'm in front of an abandon house on Vick Street, where 38 year old Ann Dawson's body was discovered. The cause of death was a single gunshot wound to the head. A homeless woman, who would like to remain nameless, stumbled across the body trying to find a place to sleep at for the night. Ms. Dawson leaves behind a son. Police has no motive of why someone would do such a thing but if anyone has any information, police urges them to contact them on the crime stoppers hotline," the reporter concluded. "When will this stop."

"NOOOOO," T.J. cried out in disbelief as tears streamed down his face. Thoughts of his life began to flash through his head as he thought about how he got to this point in his life. After falling back onto his bed, T.J. reached under his pillow and grabbed the

38 Special that was hidden there before saying a silent prayer. When he finished, he placed it in his mouth, closed his eyes and said four words, "Blood in, blood out." right before he pulled back on the trigger.

*   *   *

"What a waste of talent," Kevin said to himself as he got up and headed out of the room behind his uncle.

When Kevin walked in to the next room, there was only one casket that occupied it. When he took his seat and looked up, he couldn't believe his eyes. In the middle of the huge stand that stood at the head of the casket, rested a big picture of the notorious J.R.

J.R. was a young ruthless hustler that lived in Kevin's apartment building. Even though he had recently moved in, he was well known for his hands, but was respected for his gun play. A lot of his victim found out the hard way, even innocent ones. He welcomed all "BEEF" with open arms when other so called killers ducked and hid from it. Kevin couldn't wait to hear the story of his demise.

J.R.

On My Block

"Ay yo nigga. What the fuck you doing slanging yo shit on my block?" Mack based on J.R. as he walked up on him with two of his home boys by his side.

"Here we go again," J.R. thought. When he looked around and realized that Mack was talking to him, he wished he would have brought his banger on the block with him. He decided to leave it at home since the block had been hot for the past few days. He didn't want for the Po-Po to hem him up with dope and a banger on him. That was sure to spell FED time if he did. J.R. couldn't believe Mack had the nerve to step to him on some beef shit. There was no way J.R. could or would push his pride to the side. He figured Mack had to have a gun on him to come out of his mouth like he was doing, that or he had a death wish. Either way J.R. knew that he wasn't built like that and he was just about to prove it. "Who the fuck you talking to nigga?" he barked.

"You lil nigga," J.R. let out a slight chuckle as he walked up in J.R.'s face. He had to look down at J.R. since he was a few inches taller.

"I know what, BIG MAN," J.R. shot back, tired of all the lip boxing. "Since you've suddenly grown a set of balls all of a

dden, let's see you throw me off of YOUR BLOCK." Mack not
eing the type to back down from a challenge began to take off his
atch and necklace. A small circle began to form around the two
s they waited for the fight to start. Mack was really hoping J.R.
as going to back down and just leave the block once he saw his
vo home boys by his side but he didn't and now it was too late to
nink about the what ifs. "I ain't got all day," J.R. insisted
imping up and down in one spot throwing his head from side to
ide. The mere sight of J.R.'s fighting stance gave Mack the
ubble guts. They squared off and began walking the small circle.
R. was much smaller than Mack but a lot faster and stronger.
Aack realized how strong J.R. actually was when J.R. dodged the
rst jab he threw and countered with a left hook to his kidney that
ent him down on one knee followed by an upper cut under his
hin that landed him flat on his ass. "Get yo ass up," J.R.
emanded. He believed in giving a man a fare fight so he stepped
ack to let Mack gain his composer before he proceeded with his
esson. Once Mack was back on his feet, he swung a wild
aymaker. After missing again, J.R. put on a huge smile then
inded a left jab and a right cross to each of Mack's eyes. Not
nany people knew that J.R. was a Golden Glove in Philly before
e relocated to Wilson. Mack was finding out the hard way. This
me when Mack hit the ground J.R. jumped on top of him and
ommenced to beating his fist against Macks face.

"He gonna kille'em," a bystander swore between punches. When J.R. felt like Mack had had enough, he got up and ran his pockets then spat in his face.

"This is officially my block now Pussy," J.R. declared as he slapped the side of Mack's face to wake him up. Mack looked from left to right through swollen eyes trying to figure out where he was at. He remembered once he saw his two home boys helping him up as J.R. rubbed his knuckles trying to ease them from throbbing. When Mack finally got to his feet, he held his head down in defeat and wobbled off the block.

*   *   *

When night fall came around, J.R. was still on the block pumping his rocks. As he stood in front of the corner store puffing on his blunt, he noticed an old rusted out Lumina coming up from his left side. He was glad to see it since that sell would make the last one for him for the night. So he thought. When the car came to a halt, the doors shot open and out jumped two masked men with guns in hand. "Oh shit," J.R. shouted as he dropped the blunt from his lips and took off running through the dark alley with the two masked gunmen behind him dead on is heels. He almost got away if it wasn't for the back of his pants leg getting hung up on the last fence he crossed. "Shit," he grunted as he came tumbling down the side of the fence on to the side of his face. When the gunmen caught up to him, they stood there with their guns drawn.

You can have the money," J.R. pleaded hoping the stick-up kids would be satisfied with the three grand he had on him.

"This ain't no stick-up bitch," the taller gunman announced as he took off his mask to reveal his identity. At that point J.R. knew the gunmen intended on killing him. He squinted his eyes trying to remember where he knew the guy from, then it hit him. It was Mack's older brother Malcolm.

Malcolm stood about six foot five, was well built and was known for keeping two pistols on him at all time. Word around town was that he had beat three bodies. Those were only the ones he was charged with. He had seven more in the past year alone and by the looks of things, he was about to add one more notch under his belt.

"So, I see Mack sent his big brother to handle business for him since his bitch ass couldn't huh?" J.R. knew there was no need in pleading any more by the look Malcolm had in his eyes. It was the same look he gave his victims before he ended their lives. Malcolm also had heard of J.R. and knew if he didn't end his life now that there was no way he would be able to rest, him nor his family and the words that came out of J.R.'s mouth next confirmed it. "What you waiting on mothafucka? You gonna pull the trigga or what?" It was like J.R. was begging for death and that's what Malcolm planned to give him as he let off a .38 round in to his chest. J.R. grabbed his chest and took in deep breaths as he tried to breath. With no success he slowly began to fall towards the ground. Before he could make it all the way to the ground, Malcolm sent another shot to his head. Malcolm and is partner ran off in the direction they came, leaving J.R. for dead.

J.R. laid there in silence as he watched their shadows disappear into the dark. "Are you alright?" an old lady whispered from her back door. J.R. tried to respond but his voice was barely audible. She made her way over to where he was lying and bent her head down to figure out what he was saying.

"Take the money and drugs out of my pockets," he asked the lady. He could hear the siren in the distance getting closer and closer. She reached in his pockets and headed in to her house to stash his things then came back to his aid.

Within minutes the paramedics pulled up, followed by the police. People gathered around as J.R. was put on the stretcher and into the back of the ambulance. You could hear them whispering and making small wagers on if he would make it or not and if he did how long would it be before he gets revenge on whoever did it to him. The police question bystanders one by one. After getting the same, "I didn't see anything," they packed it up and headed out.

By the time J.R. finally made it to Wilson Memorial Hospital, the paramedics had to bring him back twice. Lucky for him the bullet that caught him in his head only grazed it and the bullet that hit him in his upper chest went in and out. He stayed in the hospital a little over a week. When police came to question him about who shot him he told them that he didn't get a good look at them. There was no way J.R. was going to let Malcolm get off the hood that easy. Death was the only option for him and that's exactly what J.R. intended on giving him.

*   *   *

Ever since J.R. was released from the hospital, all he could think about was getting revenge. He couldn't even get a good nights sleep without being awaken by the sound and the flashing light coming from Malcolms gun.

J.R. sat up every minute of the day planning a way to get at Malcolm without getting caught. It was like the more he thought he more things seemed not to come out right. He grew angrier and angrier each time at each failed attempt. He knew that if things didn't go perfectly that he could end up in jail, or even worse, DEAD! After coming up blank for the forth time, he snatched his car keys off the dresser, grabbed his gat and headed for his partner Harolds crib.

Harold was the only person J.R. trusted with his life. He always had his back no matter what the situation might bring. J.R. knew he was going to need the help of a real throughbred if he was going to successfully complete his mission.

"What's up Bruh?" Harold asked after letting J.R. in. Harold had heard about the beef J.R. had and was actually waiting to hear from his homie to see how he wanted to handle it.

"I need a big favor homie," J.R. confessed as he looked him dead in the eyes.

"Just say the word and you know I got you." A smile came across J.R's face hearing what he already knew Harold would say. After running down the plan he came up with on his way over, they loaded up the back seat with a Mac-90, AR-15 and a pistol gripped pump. Once everything was set, they jumped in J.R.'s tinted out hooptie and headed to Hunt High School to pay Mack a little visit.

They arrived just as school was letting out. They found a park directly behind Macks tricked out Tahoe and waited. The plan was to follow Mack to a secluded spot, kidnap him, then make him call Malcolm to come to where they were at. Simple as that. "There he go right there," Harold pointed at the school door exit. Mack threw his Gucci bookbag over his shoulders and proceeded to his truck. J.R.'s anger began to boil as he saw the person that almost caused him his life walking like he didn't have a care in the world. At that moment J.R. reached in the back seat and grabbed the pistol gripped pump. "Yo you ain't bout to do dis shit right here are ou?" Harold asked as he put his hand on J.R.'s arm to stop him

om getting the gun.

"Watch me" he replied as he snatched his arm loose then

pened the car door. Mack was seated in the drivers seat and never

aw him coming until it was to late.

"Oh shit," Mack shouted as he put up both arms in front of him

shield his face. It was no use, J.R. pulled back on the trigger

ithout saying a word. "BOOM." Macks driver's side window

hattered on impact as the shell found its resting spot in his dome.

R. was so busy getting the pump out of the back seat that he

ever saw the young girl get in the passenger's seat. She began to

cream at the top of her lungs before J.R. looked over at her and

houthed two words. "I'm Sorry," then sent a single shot in her

irection silencing her instantly. The parking lot was in a frenzy as

ids ran for cover. J.R. jumped back in his hooptie and slowly

hade his exit as if he hadn't just committed a double homicide.

J.R. wasn't finished his mission just yet. He pulled up to the

top sign on the corner of Maplewood and Vance. Harold looked

t him as he dipped a blunt in the half empty bottle of "BOAT,"

urned the blunt upside down, then lit it. He took a long drag as he

hade a right down Vance. When he found the house that he was

ooking for, he handed the half a blunt to Harold and got out the

ar. "What in the fuck is this nigga up to now?" Harold wondered as J.R. walked up to an old lady on the porch sitting in a chair with a blanket over her lap knitting a sweater.

"Hey baby, how can I help you?" she asked with a smile on her face.

"I hate to bother you, but I need for you to give your son a message for me," J.R. replied returning a smile.

"Sure. What is it baby?" J.R. removed the 454 Bulldog from his back and pressed it against the old lady's forehead.

"Tell Malcom I said I'll meet him in hell." The old lady never stopped smiling, she just closed her eyes then spoke.

"I forgive you baby," she told him right before he put a bullet in her head. Her head jolted back from the impact and sent her crashing out of her chair and on to the porch. J.R. walked off as a pool of blood surrounded her body. By the time he got back to the car, Harold was shocked and in a daze.

"Yo why you kill their momz man, damn," he asked as J.R. started the hooptie back up.

"Man fuck her!" J.R. shouted as he snatched his blunt back from Harold and took a long pull. Harold knew J.R. was going way to far but knew not to say anything. There was no telling what was going through his head at the time. He definitely didn't want to tick him off and be the next victim. Harold was just ready get everything over with, so he could go home and be through with him.

After riding all night through the hoods looking for Malcolm and coming up empty, J.R. decided to call it a night and continue his search tomorrow. Once he dropped Harold back off at his place, J.R. decided to make one last stop before going in.

J.R. pulled up on the block that he delivered the beat down to Mack on then killed the engine and hopped out the hooptie. A smile crept on his face as he stood back and remembered his handy work he put in. That was until he turned his head to his left and visioned the old Lumina pulling up to the corner where he stood slinging the last bit of his rocks. He watched the car pull up then two masked men jumped out with guns in hand. After watching the gunman give chase to the past him, J.R. followed behind them.

Once he got to the fence that he had tumbled over he stood to the side and watched the night of his shooting play out. The longer he watched, the madder he got. He clenched his fist tightly when Malcolm let off two rounds into his body before him and his partner took off through the alley the way that they had come from.

"I see you made it back," he heard a frail voice call out to him. It was the elderly woman that called the ambulance for him on that unforgettable night. J.R. turned and looked at the lady open up her screen door and step out onto her back porch. J.R. made his way to the opening at the door to the fence that surrounded her house.

75

"I believe this belongs to you." She handed J.R. a brown paper bag. When he looked inside, he saw the drugs that he had as well as his money that she took off of him that night. J.R. took a few hundred-dollar bills from the knot and handed it over to her. "Oh no dear. I couldn't take your money," she declined with a smile.

"No Ma'am. This is the least I can do for you taking it off of me," J.R. told her and tried handing it to her again.

"You want to pay the old lady back?" she asked, still smiling. "Well take care of yourself and I'll consider us even," she told him then turned on her heels to go back into her house.

"What's you name?" J.R. asked as she reached for the handle to the screen door. The old lady stopped and turned back around and walked to the edge of the porch. After spitting out a mouth full of snuff juice, she answered him.

"Everyone around here calls me Granny Wanny."

"Granny Wanny," J.R. looked to the ground and repeated the name trying to remember where he had heard it from before, then it hit him.

Granny Wanny was something like a Legend in the hood. She always watched out for the local dealers around the neighborhood and alerted them when the police were coming. Ever since a crooked cop robbed and killed one of her grandkids, she vowed to look out for all of the young black lives that she could.

When J.R. looked up, Granny Wanny was nowhere to be found. The crazy part of it all was when J.R. looked up at the old house that she had come out of earlier, it was boarded up and looked like it had been that way for years.

After making his way back through the alley, J.R. hopped in his hooptie and headed back to his apartment.

On his way home, he had sobered up a little and started to regret what he had done to Mack and Malcolm's mother. "Oh well," he concluded then grabbed the left over dipper out of the ashtray and lit it back up.

*   *   *

When J.R. stepped in to his apartment and turned on the lights, his heart skipped a beat. There stood Malcolm in the middle of the living room floor with eight of his most loyal soldiers. Before J.R. could reach for his strap, he felt the barrel of a gun press against the side of his dome. "Go ahead nigga," the ninth and final soldier begged through clenched teeth, itching to knock his brains out of his head. J.R. put his hands in the air as Malcolm walked up to him and relieved him of the weapon he had concealed in his waistline. Malcolm shook his head from side to side as the two killers exchanged stares. Before any words could be spoken J.R. hawked up a mouth full of flim and spat it in Malcolm's face. Malcolm put a big smile on his face as he wiped his face with his left hand. J.R. knew he was crazy when he licked his fingers afterwards then punched him in the jaw. Before J.R. could retaliate, Malcolm's goons were all over him.

When J.R. came to, he was tied to one of his kitchens chairs in the middle of the floor. "Sleeping beauty has finally decided to join us fellas," Malcolm joked before punching him in the kidney, making him lean forward in pain. When J.R. gained enough strength to lift his head, he looked up into Malcolm's eyes as one of the goons cell phone rang. Malcolm was just about to start to bring torture down on J.R. when the goon interrupted him.

"Phone Boss." He looked to his right as the Goon extended the phone to him.

"Don't you see I'm busy Fool? Take a fuckin message," Malcolm based on the Goon clearly showing his anger.

"I think you want to take this Boss," the Goon insisted. Malcolm snatched the phone away from his Goon and gave him a menacing stare. The Goon backed away not wanting to feel the wrath of his Boss.

"What?" Malcolm yelled in to the phone once he put it to his ear. He was half way through the call when he looked over at J.R. That's when everyone in the room noticed tears come from Malcolm eyes. Before the caller could finish telling him the information, Malcolm dropped the phone, walked up to J.R., and in one swift motion he pulled out a butterfly knife and slit his throat.

R.'s eyes grew as big as golf balls as he stared up at Malcolm. A nile managed to cross J.R.'s face before Malcolm pulled out a istol gripped .357 and knocked his brains out of his head clean cross the room. As Malcolm was about to leave he unloaded the est of the bullets into J.R.'s face. It wasn't until a few days later fter someone complained of a foul odor coming from his oartment before his body was discovered by the landlord.

*   *   *

"Damn," Kevin thought as his uncle removed his hand from on p of the casket and made his way out to the next room. "So those ere the shots I heard that night," Kevin thought to himself.

Kevin walked in to the next room and couldn't believe his eyes. This shit gets deeper and deeper." He stood beside is uncle and ooked down at his old friend Torey.

Torey grew up in the same building that Kevin had grown up in. orey wasn't known for getting in any type of trouble, so Kevin ondered what landed him in one of the worse places. "I guess veryone has their own little secrets," he thought to himself as he ook a seat and prepared himself for the story he was about to hear.

"I guess it's true when they say that stress kills," Freddie stated efore going in to the story.

Torey

Stressed Out

Torey was a security guard for the largest tire plant in the state. He'd been working the same job for two years, ever since he graduated high school but lately he'd been coming in late and tonight was no different. "Baby what time is it?" Torey asked his girlfriend Tahira as he quickly sat up in bed. She turned and looked on the nightstand at the alarm clock then responded.

"12:15."

"Fuck," he shouted then jumped out of bed searching for his uniform. This would make the fourth time in a single month that he was going to be late. He was glad that the supervisor was Tahira's uncle, but even he had a breaking point. Torey knew that going over her house for what she called a "quicky," was going to cause him to be late. He was never able to fuck her without falling asleep afterwards. Tahira watched him scramble like a chicken with its head cut off until he was dressed. After sliding on his shiny shoes, he darted for the door.

"Ain't you forgetting something?" Tahira asked as she sat indian-style in the middle of the bed. He ran over to the bed and eaned over to give her a kiss. "Thanks Bae but I wasn't talking bout that silly." She held up his car keys and dangled them in the ir then put them behind her back. He playfully jumped on top of er and began tickling her until she couldn't take it anymore and ave them to him. He snatched them from her hands and rushed to he door before she could retaliate.

On his way to the car all he could think about was how much he oved Tahira. They had been together for two and a half years now nd things between them couldn't have been any better. He loved he fact that she didn't have any kids and unlike most women he lated in the past, she had her own.

Torey pulled up to the front gate and punched in his four-digit ode. After trying two more times and the gate not opening, he ressed the speaker button on the side for Carl to open the gate. Once it was opened Torey headed to his station to relieve Carl of is duty.

"Sorry I'm late Ruffin. I had a little car trouble tonight." Carl ave him a look that let him know he didn't have to lie to him bout why he was late. They both started laughing as Carl athered up his belongings to go home. Before he could finish, the elephone rang. Carl was about to answer it until Torey waved him off. "I got it," he told him not wanting to hold him up any longer. "Hello. Yes. I'll be right there." Torey hung up the phone with a worried look on his face.? "Who was that?" Carl asked breaking the moment of silence.

"That was the supervisor. He told me to come to his office." They both knew that couldn't be good. The only reason the supervisor called anyone to his office was for a raise or to fire them and in Torey's case they both knew what the call was for. Carl began to unpack his things, preparing to pull a double as Torey walked out the door.

When Torey walked in to the supervisor's office, it didn't take long for him to get to the point. "There's no need to have a seat because this won't take long. "Torey stood back to his feet. "This is the fourth time this month that you have been late."

"I can explain Mr. Bowler," he began but was cut off.

"There's no need. You can pick your last check up on Friday." There was no need to try to protest because he knew his mind was already made up. Torey turned around and stormed out of the office and slammed the door behind hm. He didn't even stop by the station to let Carl know what happened, instead he jumped in his car and headed home.

When he got there, he stayed up most of the night trying to figure out how he was going to tell Tahira that he had lost his job that she stuck her neck out to her uncle to get him. Not only that, he wondered how he was going to pay all the bills in the months

hat were to come. He had saved ten thousand dollars in his bank
ccount but that was suppose to pay for his books when he went
ack to college next semester. The more he tried to come up with
 plan the more stressed out he got. After calculating more bills,
e laid on the couch in the front room and dozed off to sleep.

Torey's phone had been ringing all morning. He hated that he
idn't take it off the hook after his mother called. She always
alled at a little after eight o'clock to make sure that he made it
ome from work safe. He picked up the phone and looked at the
isplay screen to see who was calling. A smile spread across his
ace when he saw Tahira's name come up. "Hey Baby."

"Hey you. Watcha doin?" she shouted in a sing song melody.

"Missing you. What you up too sounding happy this morning?"
No matter what mood Torey was in, hearing Tahira's voice always
made him feel better.

"I got a surprise for you so when you get dressed stop by my
ouse." Torey hated surprises.

"What is it?" he wanted to know.

"You'll find out when you get here. And don't take forever
either," she shouted then ended the call. He looked at the phone
nd shook his head. After putting it on the charger, he headed to
he bathroom and took a shower.

A hour later he was letting himself in to Tahira's house with his key. "I'm in here," she shouted from the bathroom.

"I hope you ain't taking a shit,' Torey joked as he walked up to the bathroom door.

"Boy bring yo ass on in here." He reluctantly cracked the door open and stuck his head in and saw her standing in the middle of the floor smiling with one arm behind her back.

"So what's so important I had to rush out of my beauty sleep to come over here?" he joked as he walked up to her trying to see her back. He gave her a kiss on the lips then she answered.

"This!" she replied as she held up a pregnancy test. "We're going to be parents," she squealed in excitement as she began running in place. Torey was in shock as he looked at the plus sign on the stick. He didn't know what to say. "What's wrong?" Tahira asked once she saw the blank expression Torey wore on his face.

"Baby we need to talk." He walked over to the stool, put the lid down then took a seat. Tahira's heart dropped to the pit of her stomach as he grabbed her hands and pulled her to him. She hoped and prayed he wasn't about to tell her that he wasn't ready to be a father. "I lost my job last night." She removed her hands from his and put them on each side of his face.

"I already know," she replied then leaned in to kiss him.

84

"You not mad at me?"

"Of course not." Those words took a lot of weight off his shoulders. He just knew she was about to go off on him.

"I promise I'll find a job as soon as possible. Don't worry bout a thing. I'm here for you," he vowed. He stood up and held er in his arms. Before they knew it, he had her bent over the athroom zinc hitting it from the back.

*   *   *

Two months had passed and Torey had yet to find another job. veryday when he got up he would jump straight on the computer nd fill out applications on-line then head out to every place that upposed to had been hiring in the Wilson Daily Times only to ear the same old three lines, "We're only accepting applications the time, we'll call you, or his favorite line, your over qualified or the position." Tahira was more crankier than ever now. If she asn't constantly demanding him to go to the store for a craving ie had, he was buying things new for the baby. Something in his pinion wasn't necessary at the time. Torey had to get a job and on or figure out a way to get some quick cash because his bank ccount was evaporating at a steady rate.

"Ay what up Cuzo?" Dee-Dee asked once Torey answered his hone. The sound of Dee-Dee's voice was like music to Torey's ars as he hoped his prayers just been answered.

Dee-Dee was Torey's first cousin on his dad's side. Coming u[p]
they were inseparable, that was until Dee-Dee began to hang with
the wrong crowd and got turned out to the street life. On top of al[l]
that he had a very bad habit of lying but at this point he was
Torey's only option on coming up on some quick cash.

"Nothing much. What's up with you?"

"Ain't shit. Just trying to make it."

"I know that's right, me to," Torey threw in the comment.

"You driving?" Dee-Dee asked getting to the reason of his call.
For the first time Torey was glad he was calling him for a ride
somewhere.

"Yea, where you need to go?"

"On the south side of town to drop something off. You think
you can run me over there right quick?"

"Yea, give me about 30 minutes." After Dee-Dee agreed they
hung up. Torey was excited because he knew the ride to the south
side meant that Dee-Dee was going to hit him off with at least two
hundred dollars, or maybe more. Torey never dealt in drugs but
being around it and his cousin excited him, besides he really
needed the money at this time.

He picked Dee-Dee up 30 minutes later as promised and was on his way. "I really appreciate this Cuzo," Dee-Dee admitted as he it up a blunt.

'Don't mention it." Half way through the ride across town Dee-Dee looked over at his cousin through glassy eyes.

"I heard you lost your job."

"Damn everybody and they mama know I lost my job," Torey thought to himself as he answered. "Yea, and that ain't the half. Tahira's pregnant.

"Word?"

"Word!"

"So what you doing for income?" Dee-Dee wanted to know, willing to help his cousin out any way he could. As a matter of fact he was kind of glad because he knew Torey would make as many runs as he wanted him to now.

"I'm waiting on a few jobs to hit me back as we speak, but you know how that is. I been waiting on that call for a couple of months now."

"Well you know you always can work for me, that is until one of dem gigs call you, you feel me?" Torey was glad to hear those words. There was no way he was going to turn that easy money down.

"When do I start?"

*   *   *

A few more months had passed, and Torey no longer looked for a job since Dee-Dee kept his word and had steady runs for him to make. The runs paid him more than any job he had ever worked and he didn't have to work half as hard to make it. It was on this particular run that Torey and Dee-Dee ran into a little problem.

"Damn," Torey shouted in a hush like tone when he spotted the police cruiser get in behind them. "We got company." Dee-Dee began to stuff the ziplock bag filled with ounces of crack into the pocket of his hoodie. Lucky for him he knew every side street and cut in the area so getting away would be and easy task.

"Yo Cuzo, if he put on the blue lights I'ma need for you to turn the next corner at a slow pace so I can jump out and run with the dope, you got it?" Dee-Dee instructed as he grabbed the door handle.

"I got it," Torey replied as he kept his eyes glued to the rearview waiting for the police to pull them. "What if they ask who you are?"

"Just tell them a fake name and let them know you were just giving me a ride across town." After getting their plan together the police turned on his lights. Torey nervously slowed his car down and bent the next corner. Right before he could come to a

88

omplete stop Dee-Dee bailed out and took off between two
uildings like a bat out of hell. If it wasn't for Torey already
nowing the plan he would have never seen Dee-Dee take off. The
fficer knew that there was no need in running after Dee-Dee so he
ook the easy route and pulled out his gun and demanded Torey to
ut his hands on the steering wheel.

After following the officer's commands and answering a few
questions the officer was about to let him go on his way. "Can I
earch the car?" the officer asked being a dick head. Torey knew
e had nothing to hide so he gave him consent. "This is just for
ny safety," he told Torey as he put him in cuffs and sat him on the
ood of his cruiser. As soon as the officer opened the passengers
oor, the first thing he saw was the ounce of crack that had fell out
f the ziplock back Dee-Dee had. "Well what do we have here?"
he officer asked as he held the neatly wrapped ounce up in the air.
orey couldn't believe his eyes. He knew it was no need to say it
vasn't his. "It looks like somebody's going to jail." The officer
valked up to Torey, grabbed him by the arm then forcefully
hoved him into the back of his cruiser.

When they got to the magistrate's office, the officer painted a
icture as if Torey was a kingpin. He also told how his partner in
rime eluded him on foot with the rest of the dope. Needless to
ay, the magistrate was mad and hit him with a fifty thousand
ollar bond, which meant once he paid that he would only have

five thousand to his name. "There goes my college plan," he thought to himself as he made a call to the bondsman.

After calling Tahira and giving her his information to use his debit card, she came to meet him and the bondsman.

The next couple of days he called around to every lawyer's office in town to see if any of them could get the case thrown out. There was no way he could do a day in prison for something that wasn't even his. There was only one that was talking in the price range he could afford. He scheduled an appointment for later on that day to see what the deal was.

"Mr. Barnes. I'm glad you could come in today. Please take a seat," Mr. Thomas said from behind his cherry oakwood desk. "The first thing I need for you to do is tell me everything that happened, from the beginning." Torey did just that. The only thing he left out was what he had for breakfast that day. "This is going to be a hard one Mr. Barnes." Torey took a big swallow trying to remove the frog that had formed in his throat. "But I might can help you. Let me get all of your paperwork from the officer that arrested you and I'll get back to you in a week or so." Torey agreed, stood up, shook Mr. Thomas's hand then headed for the door. "Oh Mr. Barnes, there is one more thing." Torey waited for Mr. Thomas to continue. "You can leave my fee at the front with my secretary." Torey nodded his head and went to the front.

"Cash, check, or charge?" the secretary asked looking up into orey's worried eyes.

"Cash," Torey responded as he hesitantly handed over three housand dollars. Once he got his receipt, he walked out the door nd headed home.

When he got home, Torey sat on the couch feeling sick to his omach. All he could think about was how he just paid Mr. homas damn near all of his savings, just to hear him say, "I might an help you." To make matters even worse, Dee-Dee wasn't nswering his cell phone now. Torey had called him at least venty times since the incident and got the same result each time, OTHING!-

Torey couldn't believe that Dee-Dee was leaving him on stuck e way he was. "I got something for that ass," he said to himself en grabbed his car keys off the coffee table at the end of the ouch then headed for the door to go to Dee-Dee's house.

After circling the block twice, Torey stopped in front of Dee-ee's. He shook his head in disbelief as he read the big FOR ENT sign sitting in the middle of the yard. He sped off down the ock, determined to find his no good cousin. After riding the half tank of gas in search of Dee-Dee, Torey's gas light came on and e beeping signal indicating that he was almost out of gas ounded. "Fuck it," Torey decided to call it quits. That was after e got some gas, of course.

"Bingo," Torey snapped his fingers against each other making snapping sound as he pulled in to the store's parking lot and spotted Dee-Dee at the check out register. He couldn't believe his luck. Torey raced to the first gas pump he reached, jumped out of his car, then ran into the store at full speed. He was in such a hurry, he left his car door wide open. "Nigga you ain't shit," Torey swore as he put his hand on his cousin's shoulder and spun him around. He was in mid swing when he realized that the guy at the counter was not Dee-Dee. "My fault. I thought you were----?" Torey began to apologize until the stranger caught him in the jaw with a haymaker of his own that sent Torey tumbling into the snack isle. Torey tried to gain his balance, but before he could, the stranger ran up on him with cat-like speed and knocked him to the ground. It seemed no matter what Torey did, he couldn't get the stranger off of him. Being that Torey wasn't much of a fighter, he did the first thing that came to mind to get the mad man off him.

"Ouch," the stranger cried out as he grabbed his stomach. "You bit me mutha fucka." That was all the break that Torey needed. H jumped to his feet and sprinted out of the store.

"Aye somebody gonna pay for this shit," the cashier called out as Torey raced to his car. Instead of running around the car to get in, Torey slid across the hood like he was one of the Duke Boys. Lucky for him, he forgot to close the door behind him when he jumped out because the stranger was dead in behind him. The stranger wasn't so lucky though because when he tried to jump across the hood, Torey stepped on the gas and sent him flying through the air. By the time he hit the ground Torey was pulling out of the parking lot in traffic.

When Torey pulled back up to his apartment, he killed the engine then looked into the rearview mirror to examine his face. Other than a busted lip and a bruised ego, he would live. After going inside his apartment, taking a long hot shower to massage his aching bones, Torey climbed into bed and called it a night.

"Things gotta get better," he swore then closed his eyes in hopes of getting some much needed rest.

*   *   *

The following month had come and gone and things never got any better. As a matter of fact, things got even worse. He hadn't found a job yet, he just got hit with an eviction notice the week before, that he had yet to respond to, Dee-Dee got his number changed, Tahira was bitching now more than ever, and his lawyer, Mr. Thomas, claimed that he needed to see him as soon as possible. Torey figured that it had something to do with him not paying him the remainder of his balance since he was a few weeks behind on his payments. Torey's life was slowly tumbling down by the day. He had no idea of how much longer he would be able to take it before he gave up.

After forcing himself out of bed, Torey went into the bathroom to take a shower. He knew that he had to deal with one of his life situations, so he decided to start with going to see Mr. Thomas. Once he was dressed, he talked himself into taking the dreadful ride downtown to see how his case was developing, also to pay the rest of the money he owed.

When Torey walked outside he almost past out. Not because the heat index was right at 100 degrees but because he saw that his car was no longer parked in his parking space. Instead of panicking he just turned around and went back in the house. He didn't even bother calling the police since he figured the repo man finally caught up with him since he had been ducking him the previous two months. He went into the kitchen cabinet, grabbed the half empty gallon of gin, and found a comfortable spot on the living room sofa and started his day. For the last few weeks him and the bottle had become the best of friends.

Two hours into his drinking session, his telephone began to ring. He had no intentions on getting off the couch to answer it so he let the answering machine pick it up. "Hey Bae, please hurry and come over. I think it's time," Tahira shouted in pain. Torey didn't even budge. After rushing to her aid on several occasions for her "thinking" it was about that time, he was tired of making trips to her house. All she ever wanted was for him to go to the store for one of her cravings. It was like it would ring every five minutes. Even his lawyer had called a time or two to see if he was still coming in to see him. When it finally stopped ringing so did Torey's drinking. Not because he wanted to but because the bottle was empty. "Fuck this shit," he cried as he staggered the living room closet. He pulled out an old shoe box that contained his .38 special his father gave him for his security job. After retrieving it, he made his way back to his spot on the sofa. Tears streamed down his face as thoughts of what his life would be like in a few months after he went to court. "I can't go to prison," he said out loud as he placed the barrel to his head.

"Do it you worthless piece of shit," one side of his conscience was telling him.

"Don't do it Torey. Think about Tahira and your unborn baby on the way," the other side begged of him.

"Man fuck all that. What can you possible give a baby? You barely taking care of yourself!"

"Torey, you have your entire life ahead of you. Things will get better, trust me."

"Look man. You're about to go to prison for some shit that wasn't even yours, so your kid is going to be calling somebody else daddy and that's if it's really yours in the first place." Torey began to sob uncontrollably at the thought of not being there for his unborn. He knew first hand how hard it was to come up without a father figure in his life.

"I'm probably better off dead," he mumbled as he put the barrel of the gun in his mouth.

"Torey, Tahira loves you with all her heart. She believed in you when no one else did. Don't let her down." That was true. She showed him plenty of times and Torey realized it. He was pulling the gun out of his mouth just as the telephone rang, causing him to pull on the trigger. "BOOM." The bullet from the .38 Special went in to his mouth and out the back of his head, knocking his brain on the wall behind him.

"Please leave your message after the tone, BEEP."

"I'm about to leave the office for the day," Mr. Thomas voice sounded on the answering machine. "I wanted to tell you face to face but I guess this will have to do. I'm kind of in a hurry, but anyway, your case has been dismissed since your cousin was picked up last night on a drug related case and he confessed to the dope that was found in your car. I guess you were telling the truth," Mr. Thomas chuckled. "I saved the best news for last. You can come by and pick up half of your money. I have to go now. I hope you have a blessed weekend. See you soon." As soon as he hung up it rang again.

"Please leave a message after the tone, BEEP."

"Hey Baby. I just had our son. He looks just like you. He even as your brown eyes. I named him Torey too. Hurry up and get ere. This is the happiest day of my life. I love you."

Freddie shook his head and walked out of the room with Kevin ght behind him. They made their way to the front room that evin had entered when he first arrived at the funeral parlor.

When Keven entered the front room with the two caskets up ont, he couldn't believe his eyes. Not even once in all the years eeing his uncle at work had he seen him with tears in his eyes. He idn't cry at his own mother's funeral. Kevin figured it had to be omeone very close to his uncle inside the black and gold casket. evin took a seat in the corner to get ready for the best story yet. Damn, Lil Kee-Kee," Freddie began as the floodgates broke ose.

Lil Kee Kee

LOVER'S TRIANGLE

"Sneaky ass Bitch," Lil Kee-Kee thought to himself as he watched his girlfriend Diann Gucci handbag light up for the third time since she picked him up. She was praying that he didn't notice it but as soon as she made a right turn into the service station she found out that her prayers went unanswered. "Yo, you aint' gonna answer your phone?" She glanced down at her handbag as if it was her first time noticing her phone flashing on the inside. She purposely put it on vibrate because she knew how jealous Kee-Kee had become lately. As soon as she attempted to answer it, it stopped flashing. "It must be mighty important because it has been going off ever since you picked me up," he informed.

"It probably won't nobody but Tyashia and dem calling to see i I can take them to "Da O" tonight. You know dem broke ass bitches ain't got no car and shit," Diann nervously responded hoping that he bought her lie.

"Yea I bet," Kee-Kee shot back after he sucked his teeth and twisted his mouth to the side. "Don't you think it's about time for you to sit yo ass down somewhere and stay out of everybody's club?" Diann glanced down at her stomach as she waited for the car in front of her to pull away from the pump.

"Come on Kee-Kee. I ain't even showing that much so I don't
see why your're trippin." That was true. At seven and a half
months, you could barely see the small bump in her stomach she
tried so hard to keep concealed in her two sizes to small jeans. At
times Kee-Kee wondered if she had a yeast infection or if the baby
she was carrying could even breathe. The real reason why Kee-
Kee didn't want her in the club scene or out of his sight was
because he didn't trust her any further than he could see her. All
of that went out the window when he got word that Diann and his
old right hand man Hitem-Up were creeping in different places
behind his back. On top of that, it was around the same time she
came up pregnant.

"Lil Kee-Kee and Hitem-Up were two best friends that came up
in the same hood together. Unfortunately, one night inside of Club
Oscar's , Kee-Kee ran into one of his arch rivals that were in his
feelings about Kee-Kee fucking his baby mama. "Yo, what's up
with you and that bitch ass nigga Scooter. He kept mean mugging
you all night like he want it," Hitem-Up asked his partner as they
made their way outside of the club to Kee-Kee's E-300 Benz
parked in the lot on the side of the club.

"That nigga don't want it no more," he laughed, remembering
the last time he tried to run up on him. Kee-Kee threw the same
two piece combination that dropped him the last time they met up.

"That's probably why he still so mad!" Hitem-Up joked as he watched Kee-Kee bob and weave like he was in a boxing ring. "Watch out," Hitem-Up yelled out, startling Lil Kee-Kee, making him reach for the Snub Nose .38 that he had concealed in his waistline. "I was just fuckin wit you" Hitem-Up laughed when Kee-Kee pulled it out.

"Don't play like dat dawg!" Kee-Kee warned then put the gun back in its rightful place, then joined in laughing with his partner.

"You know I had your back and wouldn't let nothing like that happen," Hitem-Up responded truthfully then lifted up his shirt, showing the pearl handle of the new pistol grip .357. He was dying to use it.

Once Lil Kee-Kee made it to his car, he pulled out his keys and hit the alarm button and unlocked the doors. As soon as Hitem-Up hopped in on the passenger's side, the first thing he did was reach over into the back seat and grabbed the cd case. He bobbed his head up and down when he found the cd that he was looking for. "The Infamous Mobb Deep," he read the cover. He knew that cd would get the parking lot jumping once the bass came through the two 15' sub-woofer's that Kee-Kee had just installed. After finding the right song, Hitem-Up turned the volume up as loud as it would go, and just like he predicted, females on their way to their cars stopped in front of the Benz and shook what their momma's ave them. Hitem-Up leaned back in his seat and enjoyed the how while his partner booked chick after chick.

Lil Kee-Kee was so caught up on macking one of the hickenheads that had stopped in front of his car, he didn't even ee Scooter creeping up between his benz and the Pathfinder that at beside it. Lucky for him, Hitem-Up always stayed on point. ust as Scooter put one in the chamber and raised his gun arm up to ake aim at Lil Kee-Kee, Hitem-Up let him have it. BOOM... The ound serenaded through the parking lot, making bystanders run or shelter. The chickenhead talking to Kee-Kee wasn't so lucky ecause before Scooter's body hit the ground he let off a single hot that caught her in the back of her head, knocking her into Kee-Kee's arms.

"Come on let's be out," Hitem-Up shouted, snapping his partner ut of his trance. Lil Kee-Kee gently laid the pretty chickenhead own to the ground then jumped in his whip and pulled off out of he parking lot.

Do to the local snitches in the city, it didn't take the police long o find out who was behind the young chickenhead's killing nor who shot the guy that shot her. Hitem-Up was arrested for hooting Scooter who survived the shot in his side but was charged with murder. Since Hitem-Up's lawyer convinced the D.A. that Iitem-Up acted in self defense, his charges were dropped to nlawful possession of a firearm which got him two years at

Morrison Youth Institute. During that time Lil Kee-Kee quickly climbed his way up the food chain in the game. Upon Hitem-Up's release back into society, Kee-Kee was at the gate to pick him up in a brand new S-500 Benz, new clothes, two bad chicks and a lot of brand new money. Hitem-Up showed his boy some love before hopping in the backseat with one of the chicks. After topping him off, she helped him changed clothes.

The next day Lil Kee-Kee picked up Hitem-Up from the chicks house and had breakfast at The Pancake House and ran down everything that had changed since he'd been away. By the time they were finished eating, Hitem-Up had the new position of a General in the crew. Lil Kee-Kee knew their were going to be a lot of upset people in the crew but Hitem-Up was his man and who ever didn't like it could handle it however they wanted to handle it

A few months had passed since Hitem-Ups release and to Lil Kee-Kee's surprise, everything couldn't have been going any better. That was until Lil Kee-Kee had to take a trip out of town to re-up with the new connect. Diann had been calling him all morning, crying about she needed some money. Tired of her whinning, Lil Kee-Kee called Hitem-Up and told him to go by Dianns place and drop a few hundred off to her. When he arrived and knocked at her door, she answered it wearing a short halter top that revealed the bottom half of her breast and a pair of boy shorts with her ass cheeks hanging out of them. Lust filled Hitem-Up's es and before he left, he had her bent over the arm of the chair itting her from behind. Once word got back of their betrayal, ee-Kee confronted Diann about the accusations but she denied em just like he knew she would. He knew his main man item_Up wouldn't lie to him. They had shared many women on ifferent occasions but when he was confronted, no words were xchanged, only bullets. Since that day, they shot at each other on ght.

"You need anything outta the store?" Diann asked snapping Lil ee-Kee from his flashback. Without answering her question, he ent into his pocket and pulled out a fifty dollar bill then handed it her. Diann rolled her eyes after snatching the money from Kee-ee's hand then headed into the store to pay for the gas. As soon Diann walked into the store, she realized that she had left her andbag in the car. "Damn." She cursed herself. She looked back ut to the car and saw Kee-Kee getting out to pump the gas so she ished down the isles grabbing everything she went in for then urried to the counter to pay for them and the gas. She hoped and rayed her phone didn't go off again before she was able to get ack to the car. That was sure to be another argument she couldn't fford to have at the time. If she did, she knew Kee-Kee wasn't oing to give her any money when she asked him for it when she ropped him back off at home.

Lil Kee-Kee was halfway through pumping the gas when he looked between the front seats and saw Diann's handbag lighting up again. He quickly leaned through the front window and picked through it until he found her phone. "Just like I thought," he said to himself as he looked at Hitem-Up's name on the display screen. "Lying ass bitch," he cursed then slid her phone back in her handbag, leaned back out the window and placed the pump back on the hook. On his way back to the passengers side to get in, he noticed Diann coming out the store in a hurry. He played it off as if everything was cool but deep down inside he was furious. Leaving out of the gas station they were almost sideswiped by a big body Benz that raced to the pump for some gas. The driver looked familiar to Kee-Kee but he was too upset to figure out who he was.

After driving Kee-Kee around for about two hours making runs and picking up money, Diann drove him back to his apartment. When she parked, the questions began. "You still fucking him ain't you?"

"Fucking who?" Diann asked caught totally by surprise.

"Bitch. You know who I'm talking about," he shouted no longer able to keep his composer. They had been over this same conversation plenty of times in the past and they all started the same way.

"Oh Lord. Here we go again with this stupid shit. You always accusing me of something without even knowing the truth. Who am I supposed to be fuckin now?" she asked throwing both hands in the air in defeat. Seeing her go into her little tantrum, Lil Kee-Kee felt the temperature of his blood begin to boil.

"Come on with all that theatrical shit bitch. You know damn well who I'm talking about. Do I need to spell his name out for you?" he asked before spelling Hitem-Up's name out for her. "Remember him? If you don't let me refresh your memory. He was my right hand man, my best friend." He paused to let his words sink in her head. "The nigga that I been having shootouts with for the past seven and a half months. Do you remember him now?" Kee-Kee threatened before crashing his fist into the dashboard of her car. Kee-Kee was beyond heated but that never stopped Diann for adding fuel to the fire.

"Nigga you can miss me with all that rah rah shit," she fired back with her hand up in his face. "And you need to watch who you calling a bitch." Kee-Kee couldn't believe the heart that Diann displayed. Diann could see that she had hit a major button when she stared into his eyes, but she pressed on anyway. "You see a bitch, hit a bitch," she threw in one last remark, a remark that she would soon regret.

"Who the fuck you think you talking too BITCH?" His voice boomed through the car right before he hauled off and back handed her across her face and grabbed a hand full of her weave. After getting no response, Kee-Kee let her go but not before slinging her head into the driver's side window. "Just like I thought." Diann grabbed the back of her head and bobbed it up and down.

She stared directly into Kee-Kee's eyes with a menacing smile on her face. "And you better wipe that smug off your face before I do it for you," Kee-Kee warned, pressing his pointer finger to the middle of her forehead with each word.

"EWW, I HATE YOU SO MUCH," Diann screamed and balled up her fist. She was ready to attack but was afraid of the consequences of her actions, being that she knew she was in the wrong and he would show no pity on her when he struck back.

"I hate you more," Kee-Kee retorted before getting out of her car. He slammed the door behind him then marched up the steps that led to his apartment complex. As he went in his pocket to get his keys, he waited for Diann to hop out and act a fool as she did every other time they had a heated argument. He had to admit this time was a little different because he had never actually put his hands on her before. When he didn't hear her car door open he turned around and when he did, he saw Diann slam her fist into the steering wheel. Lil Kee-Kee instantly felt guilty for hitting her. Right when he was about to turn around and head back to Diann's car, she started it up, put it in drive and sped off down the block. Kee-Kee stood and watched as she reached the corner and if it wasn't for the elderly woman looking up, Diann would've laid her out flat at the intersection. He shook his head, turned to the door then put his key in the lock and went into the building.

$$* \qquad\qquad * \qquad\qquad *$$

After Kee-Kee changed clothes, he called his homie Mike. Mike was a little young nigga trying to come up in the game. Kee-Kee noticed his potential and decided to take him up under his wings and began showing him the ropes. Mike was a quick learner and after a few months, he had proven to be worthy of being put down with the crew.

"Yo what's the deal playboy?" Mike yelled into his cell phone over the loud music that played in the background. From the sound of things, Kee-Kee knew he had to be in somebody's gambling spot blowing money.

"Same old shit, just a different toilet," Kee-Kee responded as he slid on a pair of black Timberland boots. "I need for you to come run me somewhere," he informed his young soldier as he stood to his feet with his phone between his head and shoulder.

"Bet. Give me 30 minutes and I'll be right there." That's what Kee-Kee always liked about Mike. He was always reliable. Just before Mike disconnected the call, Kee-Kee could hear him holla out, "LOW BALL MUTHA FUCKA'S," then the line went dead.

Kee-Kee laughed to himself, knowing his little homie had just cheated a couple of hustlas out of a nice size pot.

Mike was there in 30 minutes just as he promised. "Where to?" he asked once Kee-Kee hoped in the passsengers seat of his car.

"Forest Hills Manor," he replied and looked around to check hi surroundings. He noticed several guys creeping into his building and figured his neighbor up in 3-B was throwing another one of hi famous lock-in gambling parties that he occasionally through ever month. He made a mental note to check it out when he got back from handling his business.

"You should've told me we were going to handle some business, I would've came prepared," Mike spoke noticing his big homie was dressed in all black.

"Nah you good lil homie. This here is personal," Kee-Kee assured him as he checked the clip to his Mac-11. Once he was satisfied, he placed it on his lap then laid his seat all the way back and zoned out. Once Mike pulled up in the apartment complex, Kee-Kee ordered him to pull all the way to the back. After Mike was sure that Kee-Kee was good, he dapped him up and headed th same way he entered.

Lil Kee-Kee made his way back to the front of the complex where his girlfriend Diann stayed then dialed her number.

What?" she barked still upset from earlier but Kee-Kee couldn't
show no signs of weakness.

"What my ass bitch. Where the fuck you at?"

"Why?"

"Because I'm on my way over to your place, that's why," he
replied. The line all of a sudden went silent for a few seconds. If
wasn't for her labored breathing, he would've thought she had
hung up on him.

"Kee-Kee I'm not there. I am on my way to pick up Tyashia
and the girls so we can go to the club. I told you that earlier,
remember," Diann asked trying to by a little time.

"Well when you drop them off at the club take your ass straight
home. I'll be there in a hour." Diann agreed but before she could
hang up, Kee-Kee shouted into the phone. "Don't have me at your
place waiting all night either," he warned.

"I won't damn," "Alright. Don't make me come to the club
and get you." Diann knew that he would stay true to his word
because he had done it plenty of times before. Before she could
protest, the line went dead. Kee-Kee counted down from ten and
just like he expected, her bedroom light came on. A couple of
minutes later, so did the living room light. He wasn't surprised
when Diann slowly looked around and stepped out onto the porch,
as a matter of fact, he wasn't even surprised when he saw Hitem-

Up exit out behind her with a blunt dangling from his mouth. Seeing it with his own eyes hurt him more than anything else. All that flashed through his mind was "is the baby even mine?" The churp from her car alarm snapped Kee-Kee out of his thoughts. He watched as Diann and Hitem-Up walked down the stairs and to her car. As soon as they got in and closed the doors behind them, Kee-Kee made his move. Just as Hitem-Up let down his window to let the smoke out, he saw a body moving in fast from the sideview mirror. With Hitem-Up being the trained killer that he was, he quickly grabbed his gun that he placed in his lap when he sat down. As soon as Kee-Kee reached in through the window to let off a shot, Hitem-Up had a surprise waiting for him dead center in the middle of his chest. Lucky for Kee-Kee, he never left home without putting on his bulletproof vest. Hitem-Up on the other hand wasn't so fortunate. The impact from the bullet that he let off into Kee-Kee's vest made Kee-Kee hold the trigger back on his Mac-11 making it let off a three round burst before he hit.the ground. The car suddenly shot in reverse as Kee-Kee rolled over and took off running. He heard Hitem-Up let off one last round before Diann's car crashed into another one behind her. Kee-Kee was once again knocked to the ground by the bullet Hitem-Up let off but he was able to roll over, get back to his feet and cut between two apartments. Once the coast was clear Kee-Kee proceeded back to his honeycomb hideout.

Lil Kee-Kee never stopped running until he made it home 30 minutes later. He swore that he was going to give up smoking when he threw himself on the couch in the living room. He laid there for several minutes trying to catch his breath. When he reached for his cell phone to call Diann to make sure that she was okay, he realized it was gone. He figured that he must've lost it in all the melee that was going on. He made a mental note to buy a new one as soon as he went out of the house again, whenever that might be. He knew it wasn't going to be anytime soon though. In the mean while he thought about all of the events that had unfolded over the months. "What in the fuck was that," he thought to himself as he heard several gunshots go off in what seemed like the next room beside him. After grabbing his gun and searching every room in his apartment, Kee-Kee peeked out the door but found no one there. "Damn I'm trippin." He shut the door behind him and sat back on the couch, hoping to calm his nerves. He knew he had to lay low for a while, at least for a few days until he found out if he had a warrant or if Hitem-Up survived the hit. The sound of the house phone startled him out of his thoughts. He looked at the caller id and immediately felt like kicking himself in the ass for not getting new batteries for it. He sat and wondered who was calling his line so late. There was no way he was going to answer it. For all he knew it could've been the police checking to see if he was home, so they could barge in and arrest him for the shooting. That was the last way that he was going to go out he thought as he

111

grabbed a chair from the kitchen table, pulled it to the window in the living room then cracked the blinds so no one could see him looking out.

The sun was rising as Lil Kee-Kee sat motionless in the same exact spot looking out his blinds. He hadn't stepped one foot out of his apartment in the past four days. Not since the night he had yet another shootout. That made the third one on the past seven and a half months. "Hold up," Kevin said to himself as he looked at his Uncle Freddie who was still standing over the casket. "This story sounds so familiar." His uncle stared back at him with tears flowing down his face freely. Suddenly a chill spread all through his body, his heart beat began to race at a rapid pace and the room slowly started to turn. He thought back to the night he and Hitem-Up shot it out in front of Diann's apartment building. He remembered Hitem-Up letting off one more shot while Diann's car raced into reverse crashing into the car behind them. Freddie walked over to Kevin and placed his hand on his shoulder and broke the news to him.

"They didn't make it nephew." Kevin dropped his head to his chest then closed his eyes. He couldn't believe Diann's blood was on his hands.

"What happened to her?" he asked to be sure his bullet was the one that took her life. For all he knew, Hitem-Up could've shot her and then himself. Pressure is a mother fucker.

"After Hitem-Up shot you in your vest, the impact from the bullet knocked you to the ground, but before you fell, you squeezed back on the trigger and let off a three-round burst from your Mac-11. The first bullet hit Hitem-Up in the neck and the other two hit Diann in the upper arm and the head." Lil Kee-Kee sat there in silence as he took in what his uncle had just told him.

"So what happened to the baby?" he asked.

"They were able to save him," Freddie informed. "He's in good hands. I'm going to raise him like my own." The last statement kind of bothered Kee-Kee.

"What do you mean your're gonna take care of him? Do the cops know that I shot them both?" Freddie removed his hand from his shoulder and walked over to the second casket.

"Come her nephew." Kee-Kee stood to his feet and made his way beside his uncle. "Look." Kevin glanced down at the body once Freddie opened the casket he realized what he was trying to say. Kee-Kee turned away and walked to the far side of the funeral parlor and stood in front of the mirror. Tears streamed down his face when he saw the entire right side of his head was blown off. "When you were running and Hitem-Up let off that one last shot before he took his final breath, it caught you in the head and killed you on the spot.

"That can't be true," Kevin thought as he turned around to face his uncle. "Well how am I here talking to you?" he questioned with a confused look on his face.

"You're here for closure nephew, also to say your good-byes!" Kee-Kee couldn't believe what he was hearing. There was no way that he could be dead. He suddenly remembered hearing the shots that he heard when he came home from the shootout the other night and realized they had to be the same one's that killed J.R. There were so many questions Kevin had for his uncle but there was no more time left for him. "It's time nephew," Freddie told him as he pointed behind him. When Kevin turned around, Diann appeared from a bright light. He knew what time it was then, so he walked over to join the only woman that he ever gave his heart to.

"We'll always be together Kee-Kee," she whispered in his ear as he held her tight. "I love you."

"I love you too." He turned around and took one last look at his uncle and smiled at the thought of everyone thinking Freddie was crazy when he use to tell them that he could talk to the dead. Now he knew the truth. "Thanks Unk," he mouthed then disappeared into the light.

"Your're welcome Nephew," Freddie assured him then bowed gracefully. Once the light faded away, Freddie reached in his pocket and pulled out the picture he took of Kevin and Diann's baby then placed it inside the casket with Lil Kee-Kee. After ying a short prayer he thought about how much he was going to iss Kevin and the time they shared together at the parlor. "I got ou," he promised then turned out the light and exited the room.

TO BE CONTINUED.....

Coming Soon

Wide-A-Wake

(Hood Tales Volume 2)

Junior

Freddie took a deep breath as he walked into the back room of the funeral parlor. Knowing he had a very long and busy day ahead of him, he gathered up his things to put the finishing touche on the bodies that were to be viewed the following day.

Just as he touched up his last client, Junior entered into the room and headed to the back to take a seat. He knew to be as quie as possible because Freddie hated to be disturbed while he was at work.

Junior was Freddie's great nephew. Freddie began raising him a little over sixteen years ago right after his nephew Lil Kee-Kee and Juniors mother Diann were both killed in a fatal shootout one night. Freddie had made a promise to raise Junior as if he was his own and that's exactly what he did.

Freddie paused and smiled when he felt his great nephew's presence. "How was school today?" he asked glancing over his

houlder. It always amazed Junior that no matter how quiet he
vas, his uncle would know whenever he or anyone else entered
nto the room.

"It was cool," he replied as he slid his bookbag from his
houlder, sat it down beside him then took a seat. Junior reminded
reddie of Lil Kee-Kee in so many ways. It was like he was
eliving old times whenever he would look in his face. Junior even
at in the same seat as his father to listen to the stories that his
ncle would tell him. Freddie shook those memories from his head
s he waited for the question his great nephew was sure to ask him.
What happened to them?" Junior asked as he reached over to the
odium beside where he was sitting and picked up the obituary and
egan flipping through the pages.

"In loving memory of Vernon Styles Jr.," it read with a big
oving picture of V.J. with his name up under it. Junior opened it
nd began to flip through the pages, waiting for his uncle to tell the
tory.

CPSIA information can be obtained
at www.ICGtesting.com
Printed in the USA
LVHW031932171019
634538LV00010B/1025/P